1989

INTERVIEWING FOR A CAREER IN PUBLIC ACCOUNTING

BY JOHN J. HIGGINS
**Second Edition Edited by
Richard L. Baird**

HAMPTON PRESS
ROCHESTER, MICHIGAN

HIEBERT LIBRARY 58593
Fresno Pacific College M. B. Seminary
WITHDRAWN
Fresno, Calif. 93702

Copyright © 1981 by John J. Higgins
Second Edition Copyright © 1989 by John. J. Higgins

All Rights Reserved

No part of this publication may be reproduced, stored in a
retrieval system, or transmitted in any form or by any means, elec-
tronic, mechanical, photocopying, recording, or otherwise,
without the prior written approval of the publisher. Approval
may be obtained from the Permissions Department, Hampton
Press.

Library of Congress Catalog Card No.: 89-84781.

ISBN 0-938352-008

Cover design by Joseph Kiwior

Published by

HAMPTON PRESS
P.O. Box 805, Rochester, Michigan 48063

Printed by Harlo Press, 50 Victor, Detroit, Michigan 48203

INTERVIEWING FOR A CAREER
IN PUBLIC ACCOUNTING

To My Family

CONTENTS

ACKNOWLEDGMENTS

A text that gives you specific information on interviewing with CPA firms cannot be written by someone unfamiliar with the profession. Therefore, I wish to acknowledge first the many thousands of accounting majors at numerous colleges throughout this great country who have unknowingly provided the knowledge required to allow me to write for their successors—tomorrow's accountants.

Rutten Welling & Company, Deloitte Haskins & Sells, Laventhol & Horwath, and Coopers & Lybrand have given me the opportunity, training, atmosphere and latitude to practice the art of interviewing.

DR. DAVID GABHART encouraged me to share my thoughts with you in writing.

My family persevered for over a year while I wrote evenings and weekends. My wife typed the first draft—no easy chore when considering the muddy condition of my handwritten draft.

ANNE KUPSTAS typed the manuscript and its many editing changes. DENNIS DiPAOLO edited—Thank God!

This manuscript was reviewed by educators, placement officers, personnel directors and students:

Dr. Alvin Arens, Dr. Harold Sollenberger, Dr. William Welke, Dr. James Pattillo, Dr. David Gabhart, Dr. Dennis

Gaffney, Mr. Vincent Kopy, Mr. Jack Shingleton, Mr. Edwin Fitzpatrick, Mr. William Spencer, Mr. William V. Allen, Mr. Robert Petz, Mr. Vince Ammann, Mr. Scott Bailey, Ms. Vicki Healey, Mr. Steve Eder, Ms. Penny Freligh, Mr. Bill Gerber, and Mr. Matt Rizik.

Thank you!

PREFACE

While this book is directed primarily toward accounting students interviewing for a career in public accounting, much of the information provided is relevant for virtually any business interview. You will be provided with:

A broad understanding of the sophisticated interview process utilized by public accounting firms and other successful businesses.

Specific suggestions to develop or enhance your interview skills.

Knowledge of the public accounting profession and its expectations.

Reading this book will not make you into something you are not, but if you have the potential to succeed, it will greatly assist you in conveying to the employer that you can play an important role in their continued success. In a sense, you are the product of a new marketing campaign. Your advance research, development of the "product" (you), attractive packaging and thorough public relations strategy is designed to earn your acceptance by the "consumer" (employer).

With a better understanding of what to expect during the interview process, you will spend less time on the form and more time on the substance of your interview. Better interviewing skills and better questioning and listening techniques will produce an employment opportunity leading to a career, not just a job.

Firms, too, will benefit by staff who are better prepared to cope with the rigors of a professional career. Interviewers will no longer see well-qualified students miss their opportunity with public accounting firms because of poor interviewing skills or ignorance.

This book reflects the real-world experiences of two interviewers who wish to share their knowledge with you. It is not a theoretical treatise on interviews, nor is it filled with statistics, graphs and charts. You know the rules of etiquette and business decorum or can gain this knowledge through publications that are available to you free of charge from your placement office. Read them!

Nearly 55,000 accounting majors will graduate from American colleges and universities this year. Of these, 17,000 will begin a career in public accounting; 38,000 will enter other careers. You and your accounting classmates will amass close to one-half million campus interviews.

GOOD LUCK WITH YOUR INTERVIEWS!!

AUTHOR'S COMMENT

To avoid the confusion of awkward pronoun patterns such as he/she or his/hers, the conventional use of the masculine pronoun to refer to both male and female has been used at times.

1 INTRODUCTION

CPA firms spend large sums of money to develop, establish and implement well-oiled recruiting machines. You, on the other hand, have been worried about Psych. 201, Cost Accounting, Dr. Jones' final exam or FASB #96. Consequently, you have spent little time and no money preparing for your interviews. The firms have a definite advantage. Effective use of this book will tend to offset the firms' advantage.

This book is your interview handbook. It provides a quick way to learn about the profession, the interview process of the profession and some of the techniques that will make you look good to an interviewer.

Interviewers will also be reading this book. Once they discover you know what to expect, they will begin to change their style, techniques and tactics. No doubt the revelations in this book will cause a stir within the profession. Great! As discussed later, change will occur and this is good for everyone involved.

Many books are written on interviewing, but none as yet have been written on the subject of public accounting interviews. The authors spend part of every day answering questions about interviewing with public accounting firms and have given many speeches not only to accounting clubs but also to accountants who want to learn how to interview. Therefore, it seemed logical to publish the information accumulated from many years of practical experience.

The information in this book will give you a fighting chance because you will have information and knowledge never before available to students.

Before going into the interview process, however, several reviewers of this work have suggested that a strong statement be made at the outset on the rigors of public accounting.

Public accounting is a business! As such, it must produce a profit for its owners, the partners, by performing certain services for clients. You, the accountant, the one who performs the services and produces the profits, will service the client when and where needed.

The service nature of the business will cause conflicts with your personal desires and will be very irritating and frustrating—hopefully, only at times. In other words, it's a profit-oriented business stressing client service before your personal needs. Plans may be changed. All firms endeavor to make your life and career a pleasure; but there will be times when client needs—not yours or your firm's—will overrule.

Realizing these uncertainties now will give you a better chance at *career* survival.

2 PLANNING YOUR INTERVIEWS

Planning is one of the most important but often the most neglected step in the interview process. Please take the time to read this chapter in detail, assimilate the information, and put it into practice—*NOW!*

INTERVIEW GOALS AND OBJECTIVES

The best place to begin a successful career search is to establish your goals and objectives. Unfortunately, some students never set a goal. Others set only one—to get a job. Ideally, you will realize that there may be several intermediate stages to be reached before attaining a final goal. When considering interviews for a career in public accounting, there are four separate objectives to be attained. Yours are:

- *Complete Preparation*—Do all that is possible to be prepared for your interviews.

- *Receive Office Visit Invitations*—This is the primary purpose of each campus interview.

- *Receive Multiple Employment Offers*—These will come as the result of your office visits.
- *Accept A Position*—If your first three objectives are met, you will then be able to decide on a firm which you sincerely believe meets your career goals.

Each objective is a complete step and must be completed in sequence toward your final goal—a position in public accounting.

As you will come to realize, the recruiting process can become a numbers game. All firms, through forecasts and budgets, determine the total number of candidates to be hired for a school year. Each firm desires to grow their practice through new business development and must project this growth as it relates to the number of people hired to do the work and maintain desirable productivity levels. Using ratios developed over the years (explained later) they fairly accurately determine the number of students to be invited for office visits and the number of offers to extend. Many offices even project goals by university. This projection process sometimes allows interviewers to set a specific number of students per interview schedule in which to express further interest.

About 25 percent of all students interviewed on campus by public accounting firms receive office invitations. Students who are serious about a career in public accounting must be among this 25 percent. The purpose of this chapter is to properly prepare you for your interviews.

CAREER GOALS

The first decision you must make concerns your career. Through three or more years of college, you have prepared yourself to be an accountant. Now it's time to begin what will be a totally new phase of your life— making the transition from the life of a student to that of a businessperson. If you have not yet decided what you want to do, decide now; or at least decide that you will give each interviewer the *IMPRESSION* that you want to spend your career with his firm or company.

If you decide on public accounting as the place to begin

your career, say it—"Career in Public Accounting." Write it on your resume and college credentials; and most importantly, develop an answer to the question "why?". The correct answer involves such areas as responsibility, training, professional career and professional challenges. "Pick your poison," but develop one of these areas (there are others too). Decide now which one fits you and prepare to sell it to an interviewer! You have no chance at a career unless you can convince people that you are serious about beginning in your chosen field. You may or may not plan to spend your entire working life in public accounting, but you must be able to give the *IMPRESSION* that public accounting is for you.

Interviewers frequently read resumes or college credential forms which state: "public or industrial accounting" as a career objective. This is a mistake! The last thing you want to do is convey an image of indecisiveness. Who wants to hire a business person who cannot make up his mind? It is better to write a separate resume for each type of interview and hand-carry it to the interviewer.

A corporate interviewer may want to know why you are not interested in public accounting. A public accounting interviewer rarely asks why you are not interested in private accounting.

ORGANIZATIONS

The organizations you join will reflect the interest you have in your chosen profession. Become a member of your campus Accounting Club, Beta Alpha Psi or other accounting organization and state it on your resume. Interviewers today look for *ACTIVE INVOLVEMENT* in campus accounting organizations. If you cannot be an officer, be a committee chairperson or at least active and visible on a working committee. Support of and involvement in an accounting-related activity on campus is a strong plus in your favor. Being a dues-paying member only for the purpose of putting it on your resume is not enough.

Be ready to explain why you have chosen not to become a member of an accounting club if such is the case.

After you have joined the accounting organization, join any other club or organization you desire and use the experience to your personal benefit.

Many students have been successful in obtaining an office visit by meeting and becoming known by interviewers at professional activities. Guest lists at these functions usually include several interviewers. Introduce yourself and begin to develop friendships, speaking to individual interviewers again on any and all possible occasions. It is difficult for an interviewer to reject someone he or she has known for six months or a year. However, do not concentrate only on one interviewer. See them all!

If it is difficult for you to be as "forward" as is suggested, perhaps you should consider a career other than public accounting. Realize that public accounting is a service business where people (businessmen and businesswomen) must be able to sell themselves to others. You should seriously question your ability to function effectively in public accounting if you are hesitant to meet interviewers who will be friendly.

FIRM LITERATURE

About a month prior to campus interviewing, each firm sends recruiting literature to the placement office of each campus. This literature, referred to as a "brochure," is for your use. Pick up a copy of each firm's brochure and study them all carefully. Realize that many firms use professional agencies and writers to paint a positive picture of their firm in these brochures.

Read each brochure to gain information, noting buzzwords used by particular firms and differences between firms. After reading several brochures, you will probably discover that *ALL* the firms are potential employers. And they are! Also, you will not be able to discern any significant differences between the firms (i.e., career path, opportunities, training, etc.). Pay little or no attention to the pictures in the brochures for you will gain no meaningful insights from them. Yes, they are beautiful and depict professionalism, family, nondiscrimination, etc., but they should not be used in your evaluation of any firm.

A student is usually asked during an interview, "What can I (the interviewer) tell you about our firm?" Many students will make the disastrous mistake of saying, "I read your brochure and it answered all my questions." This student will probably be rejected because a brochure cannot possibly answer all the questions involved in a student's decision. The literature is designed to be a broad description of the firm, not the firm itself. The brochure can be helpful in providing you with a foundation of information from which you can develop questions for your interviewer which indicate you have researched the firm. Pay attention to the way each firm labels their special service areas in consulting, EDP auditing, Microcomputer Advisory, actuarial, etc. In other words, know the "BUZZ-WORDS" for each firm.

You should also be aware that there may be tremendous differences between offices within a firm. A brochure cannot possibly describe the full range of dynamics involved in an entire organization. It makes no more sense for you to base a career decision on a brochure than for an interviewer to hire you based solely on your resume.

RESEARCHING FIRMS

We have strongly recommended going beyond the obvious (recruiting brochures) to research firms prior to the interviewing process. Thorough research helps you be more knowledgeable during the interview (thereby impressing your interviewer) and provides you with valuable information in what will perhaps be the most important decision-making process of your life.

Following are some sources which you may consider helpful:

Accounting Today—Published by Lebhar-Friedman, Inc.; 425 Park Avenue, New York, New York 10022; (212) 371-9400. $48 per year (1988). This is a weekly tabloid (newspaper format) which covers a wide variety of current events in the accounting field. Topics include accounting rules development, marketing strategies, auditor changes, mergers, software development, lawsuits and feature stories on many different subjects.

Big Eight Review—Published by The Big Eight Review, Inc.; 2824 Sahalee Drive East, Redmond, WA 98053; (206) 869-0655. $72 per year student subscription (1988). A monthly summary of selected articles from major United States financial and news publications citing the Big 8 international accounting firms. Editorials included monthly on significant issues affecting the firms and profession. Special Annual Report issue published in July each year.

The CPA Journal—Magazine published monthly by the New York State Society of CPAs; 600 Third Avenue, New York, New York 10016. $19 per year for undergraduate and graduate students, all others $38 (1988). Articles include various topics for firm management, technical and professional updates.

Journal of Accountancy—Magazine published monthly by the American Institute of CPAs; 1211 Avenue of the Americas, New York, New York 10036-8775. $30 per year (1988). Regular features include taxes, Accounting in Industry and Management Advisory Services, Practice Management, Technical Updates, technology, professional issues, government accounting and items of general interest.

New Accountant—Magazine published six times per academic year directed at the accounting college student; 33 Village Square, Glen Cove, New York 11542. Distributed free to students through accounting department offices at four year institutions. Personal subscription for student available at $8 per year, all others $20 (1987). Regular features include accounting careers, reader surveys, career advancement and professional issues of interest to college students.

Public Accounting Report—Published by Thomas F. Hatcher; P.O. Box 81067, Atlanta, GA 30366; (800) 634-2475. $197 per year (1988). Privately circulated twice monthly newsletter covers auditor changes, legal affairs, personnel moves, firm association announcements, new partners, mergers, dissolutions and withdrawals, firm acquisitions, updates on AICPA, FASB and SEC actions and miscellaneous areas.

Other research materials which often have articles pertaining to the accounting profession include the *Wall Street Journal, Forbes, Business Week* and *Fortune*, to name a few. These publications will also improve your general business knowledge.

Don't overlook the pertinent information you can obtain from talking with faculty, placement professionals, graduates of your school (even if you don't know them personally, they are flattered, in most cases, to be consulted— remember, they were in "your shoes" x number of years ago), and current students who did firm internships.

FACULTY AND PLACEMENT
OFFICE RECOMMENDATIONS

Unless an interviewer has spent an enormous amount of time on campus meeting students (most have not), the interviewer will ask faculty and placement officers for the names of outstanding students. Faculty will always be asked; placement officers will be asked on smaller campuses but less frequently as the size of the campus grows.

A strong faculty recommendation definitely enhances a student's chances in receiving an invitation to visit the office. Therefore, it is in a student's best interest to become known as a good student by several faculty members. When an interviewer shows a faculty member the list (called a "schedule") of students to whom he will be speaking that day, the faculty member will be sure to mention you as one of the students that "could" be invited into the office. It is difficult for the interviewer to resist this kind of suggestion for fear of alienating the faculty member or because the faculty member may be right—you are good!

How do you get a good faculty recommendation? By excelling as a student and by meeting and knowing your faculty personally. Support and help them! Be active in accounting department activities, the Accounting Club or Beta Alpha Psi. Also recognize that many faculty have outstanding relationships with recruiters and firms. It is not unusual for faculty members to have developed long standing friendships with firm partners and staff. Many firms provide research grants, internships, endowed chairs and other support to faculty. Your preparation should include determining the extent of such relationships on your campus.

Let's face facts. Even a mediocre interviewer can spot an outstanding student and extend an invitation to visit the office. All students, though, are not outstanding. In fact, most do not have the grades, personality and business acumen to be rated as outstanding. To the masses of "not outstanding" students, begin now to market yourself to your professors. Effort along these lines will go a long way. Interviewers have heard many times: "I had this student in Advanced; as his grades indicate, he's not the smartest but I remember him as hardworking and involved. I heard good things about him from Dr. Smith too!" What choice does an interviewer have at that point but to invite the student into the office?

A faculty recommendation will usually result in an office visit. Since your goal in a campus interview is to receive an invitation to visit an office, a faculty recommendation truly helps you. During the office visit, however, you are on your own. You must sell yourself because the recommendation only gets you into the office.

STUDENT RECOMMENDATIONS

The same type of investigation that takes place with faculty takes place with students. Campus leaders (i.e., Beta Alpha Psi or Accounting Club officers) are asked by interviewers either directly or indirectly, "Who are the best students?" Alumni of your campus, especially last year's graduates, are asked; and former and current interns who may or may not have accepted an offer are asked to recommend students.

Obviously, it is in your best interest to be known and to receive a recommendation from these "power brokers." Do not make the mistake of thinking that this is just "B.S." or "playing the game." What you are really doing is helping yourself reach a goal. If reaching your goal involves "stepping out" of yourself, do it! And be proud of it!

Always be prepared to give positive comments about faculty members and fellow students. During the course of an interview, the topic of faculty or other students may arise. You do not know who the interviewer knows and/or likes. Therefore, you should give appropriate "strokes"— fair to positive—for all. Never downgrade a faculty member or student for this is easily translated into you being a negative person who will continue to complain once hired. "He was a tough grader, but I learned a lot," is better than saying, "I was ready to kill him when he gave me that C for a grade."

LOCATION

One of the more perplexing questions facing students during an interview is that of location preference—the city in which you want to work.

If you grew up in a city, attended a local college and desire to work in that same city, you are like the vast majority of college graduates. Your location preference is easy. Tell the interviewer you wish to stay in the same city.

Usually the interviewer will also be from that city and is interviewing for the local office. Your troubles are over!

If on the other hand you wish to work in another city, you have new challenges facing you:

- there must be an opening in the office,
- the office must be willing to accept you as a referral,
- you must be an outstanding student, and
- you must be able to convince the interviewer to refer you.

Is there an opening or not? Ask! The interviewer may say "yes," "no" or may plead ignorance of the number of "remaining openings" as a hedge against committing himself to an early decision. Realize that referrals to a large office are easier and more plentiful than to a small office. Each office in a firm recruits at local campuses and fills most or all positions from local sources.

However, offices do accept referrals so as not to become too inbred with local talent. From an office's vantage point change is refreshing from time to time.

Who is referred? Usually only outstanding students or students with a special talent are referred. Interviewers often say, "That student isn't strong enough to refer to such-and-such-a-place, but I'd invite him into my office." The reason is that most students are not evaluated as outstanding. They are good enough to work for the firm in the local office, but not good enough for the interviewer to refer. The assumption is that the receiving office can find other good students through its own recruiting efforts. Therefore, why should the firm or receiving office pay several hundred or several thousand dollars (air fare, hotel, cabs, dinners, etc.) to refer students when the same quality can be found on local campuses without the additional expenses? The bottom line is that if you are not an outstanding student (and don't fool yourself with regard to what the word means) your chances of getting a referral are severely limited and you should probably consider concentrating on the local office near your home. Bear in mind that it is much easier to request and receive a transfer to another office after you have some practical experience under your belt (2 or more years).

If you consider yourself as an outstanding student, you may be able to convince an interviewer to refer you to another city. Your task is to develop sound reasons for desiring the referral. Too often students desire a referral to one of the garden spots (i.e., San Francisco, Los Angeles, San Diego, Denver, Miami, Boston, etc.) for reasons such as like the weather, like the ocean, want to ski, have friends there, etc. Needless to say, these are not good reasons for an office to accept you as a referral candidate. Additionally, and perhaps more importantly, you are asking the interviewer to put his reputation on the line with peers. If you do not receive an offer or eventually begin employment in a totally different city, the interviewer looks bad. Since interviewers do not like to be put in that situation, and because someday they may want to make another referral to that office of a truly great student, they do not want to make a mistake. You will be quizzed thoroughly on your reasons for desiring a particular city. Be prepared!

Good reasons can be personal or business, but make them convincing. For instance, good reasons are: that's home, worked there or visited there and have decided to spend my career there; have close family ties there; parents have decided to retire there; fiancee has already accepted position there; have investigated the growth opportunities available and want to take advantage of them, these opportunities are: . . . If you do not have strong personal ties with the city, develop sound business reasons.

Do not tell an interviewer that you want to work in any office anywhere, or in any office within a large geographic area. Be specific as to cities. The interviewer will not make calls to a number of offices on your behalf only to be rejected because you have no good reason to work in any of them. You are much better off if you say something to this effect: "I prefer to work in X; however, I am flexible." Say no more until you hear the interviewer's reaction. Then be prepared to give your reasons. If the interviewer's reaction is positive, you may be home free. But, if he or she hedges in any way, you should be prepared to retreat to your second choice (with reasons), the local office near your home or the office of the interviewer. Getting in the door with the firm somewhere may be better than an outright rejection.

Your credentials and resume can state your location preference. If you have an absolute preference, state it. If you are not sure or are willing to work anywhere, state "none" or "open" and be prepared to discuss your needs in the interview. Occasionally, a firm may have an office that has experienced explosive growth and cannot meet their hiring needs from normal recruiting sources, thus requesting more referrals from across the country. If you are open to relocation, say so—but you should have a specific city as your first choice.

If you are successful in obtaining a referral, do not keep it a secret. Let all the interviewers know. Let them know for several reasons:

- You may be able to interview several firms on the same trip, thus cutting the pro rata share of the expenses between the firms (a very important fact).

- You are really serious about your location preference and were able to convince someone—even the competition. Any interviewer will be impressed with this, and interviewers tend to respect one another's opinions.

- Competition between firms in the distant city may also be on your side ("we're better than they are, so let's prove it to the student").

GRADES

When interviewers arrive on campus for the day of interviews, they scan the resumes on their schedule. The only quantitative measurement is grades. Most firms will generally agree that an acceptable candidate will have a 3.0 grade-point average (GPA) (overall and in accounting) or above—the higher the better. Students below a 3.0 GPA are often rejected on grades alone. However, several Big-8 and many non-Big-8 firms will seek students or at least be interested in students below a 3.0 GPA. On some campuses even low grades are more than acceptable because of the known quality of faculty, students, programs and grading system.

Before getting much further into a discussion on grades, one point should be made very clear to everyone: most studies on the subject show no correlation between high grades in college and eventual success in the business world.

There are no hard-and-fast rules but, in times of heavy demand for students, requirements are lowered and then raised as demand lowers. For example, demand for students is lowered during a recession or as recruiting quotas near filling. It is, therefore, in your best interest to interview early in your senior year.

Students with very high grades have an excellent chance of obtaining a position in any firm. The only question raised concerning a very high GPA is not grades but rather personality. Those with very high GPAs are sometimes tagged as intellectuals who cannot relate well to people or problems on a practical level. If you have both a high GPA and a pleasant personality, you will probably receive many offers and be able to choose among them.

The vast majority of students interviewing have between a 3.0 and a 3.5 grade-point average. Students with these grades are usually acceptable to all firms. In other words, if a firm rejects you with these grades, your rejection would not be based on your GPA.

Students with lower grades should expand their job search well beyond the national firms, to regional firms and local firms. (A list of these firms can be obtained from the state CPA society, placement office or accounting faculty.) Students below a 3.0 GPA will find positions in public accounting, but must market themselves differently and more diligently. Whatever the reason (interviewers have heard all the excuses for low grades), you must be prepared to put your best foot forward. If your accounting GPA is higher than your overall GPA (it should be), state only your accounting grades. Or, if your grades are higher during your last two years, state only your highest year (i.e., "3.4 Junior Year" or "3.2 Senior Year"). Many students flounder grade-wise for a while before getting on track. It may be enough for the interviewer to see a good student with an upward trend in grades. If your GPA is low and the interviewer does not ask you about grades, he may have decided to reject you and is only going through the motions of an interview. For this reason, be proactive and bring up the subject yourself. Point out the upward trend, the difficult electives you chose, etc. Be prepared to give other examples of your mental capacity and problem solving abilities. Remember, you have nothing to lose . . . and much to gain!

Always be honest about your grades because you will be asked for an official transcript. However, there is nothing wrong with stating only your strong points. If your overall is 2.7 and your accounting grades are 3.1, just state, "3.1 in Accounting." The interviewer may find you acceptable and not probe any further. But if there is any probing into grades, be prepared to state reasons (i.e., had to work 25 hours per week, ill, sports, band, etc.), not defend your grades. If you become defensive about your grades, you will probably "dig your grave." If, on the other hand, you have sound reasons, you have a chance at a successful interview. Remember, interviewers are also reading this book.

PERSONALITY

This is an area where no book will be of much help. Your personality has already been formed, but there are some suggestions to help you prepare for your interviews.

Probably every book ever written on interviewing states that you should "be yourself" during an interview. This is the *WORST* advice that could be given to many students. To some, being yourself implies cut-offs, jeans, beer, waterskiing or whatever. To others, it means cracking the books, telling jokes or being the life of the party. Being yourself may not be what impresses an interviewer. Interviewers may not want to invite to their office students who have won the "chugging contest" or have led the "death march" or whatever else may have endeared you to your fellow students. Interviewers are looking for young businessmen and businesswomen who have demonstrated through their campus involvement the capacity to recognize issues, solve problems, motivate others, etc. Interviewers look for students with the ability to smile, communicate orally and in writing, show a genuine interest in the firm and possess curiosity and inquisitiveness.

In the phrase "public accounting" there are two words. If you will, "public" relates to personality, and is first, while "accounting" relates to grades in college, and comes second. Have acceptable grades, concentrate on a good firm handshake—women should offer their hand to be shaken—and smile. *A belief in yourself and your abilities and an interest in the firm* are the basic components of success. Be a businessperson about to embark on one of the most important decisions of your life.

When you have had several offers and are ready to make your decision, then be yourself. Relax and decide where "yourself" best fits with the people and the firm.

COLLEGE CREDENTIALS/RESUME

The placement office of most colleges asks you to register with them and complete some type of application. Many use a form designed by and used exclusively on that campus. Regardless of the form, it should be completed accurately and should include your achievements and accomplishments. Above all, make it perfect because that one sheet of paper represents you. The only impression an interviewer may have of you prior to your meeting is conveyed on that sheet of paper. It must be neat, accurate and in all respects perfect. Also, remember what was said earlier about "putting your best foot forward."

A resume is required by some placement offices and is standard fare on most campuses. Many students write their resume in a communication course. Preparing a resume is an excellent opportunity for students to organize their thoughts about the future and develop their background into a marketable package.

A resume can do many things for you. It is a snapshot (not a photo album) of your life and achievements to this point. It provides a glimpse into your thought process on organizing information and communicating. It can serve as a "road map" for both you and the interviewer, allowing for effective conversation about "what makes you tick" in a limited timeframe. It establishes you as an individual, with a set of experiences and accomplishments totally unique to you. *The College Placement Annual*, available free from your placement office, gives you excellent examples to follow; many fine books are written on the subject and available in your campus library. Follow the samples in these books and in Chapter 11. If you can afford it, have your resume professionally printed rather than just typed. Do remember that a resume reflects you and therefore must be perfect. It is a good idea to have your resume critiqued by placement professionals, faculty or other contacts you may have with individuals qualified to give you constructive criticism. One tip: read your final draft backwards which forces you to read one word at a time to spot typographical errors and avoid interview embarrassment.

WOMEN AND MINORITIES

Public accounting firms actively seek women and minority accounting majors for their staff. This is not a canned statement of Affirmative Action goals but rather a simple fact in today's business world. Also, it is a statement that was not and could not have been made prior to the early seventies.

Women represent about 50% of all new staff members entering professional positions in large firms. This percentage roughly corresponds to the number of women graduating from college with accounting majors. The number of female accounting majors has steadily increased during the 1970s and '80s. Regardless of the reasons, the fact is that women choose a career in accounting today in ever increasing numbers. To be sure, vestiges of bias still exist; but women rose to the partnership level during the '70s and will continue to gain ground in the years ahead.

While today's women entering the accounting profession or the business world in general can hardly be classified as "pioneers," interviewers realize that some bias still exists and therefore tend to lean toward females with that "rough and tumble" pioneer spirit. Successful business people are aggressive, know what they want, and possess a demeanor that allows them to take setbacks in stride. Women who have not yet cut mom's apron strings (those who fit the little-girl-next-door image) may find resistance. Be a businesswoman ready to accept the challenges offered by what is still a man's business world. Be a lady, but be a little tough too!

Male and female minority students are in demand; the supply is short. There is little question that the Civil Rights Act was an initiating factor for the increasing demand of minorities. Firms today, however, seek minority students because it makes good, sound business sense—not because of law. Minority students need not (indeed should not) interview differently from any other student.

QUESTIONS YOU SHOULD ASK

An interview, as you will learn in the next chapter, has two main parts: the interviewer's questions and the student's questions. Many students in preparing for their interviews concentrate on the questions the interviewer will ask of them and neglect or devote less time to questions to be asked of the interviewer. Your preparation *MUST* include questions to be directed at the interviewer to demonstrate that you have a genuine interest in the firm and in your career. Your questions must be intelligent and well thought out—not just a long list to be rattled off just because it's expected. Additionally, your questions can demonstrate research you have done on firms which should impress your interviewer. (Refer to page 58 for a sample list of appropriate questions and space to develop questions you may want to ask.)

Some students bring a list of prepared questions into the interview. Generally, this is received negatively by an interviewer. The interviewer questions the memory of a student who cannot remember a few simple questions for thirty minutes. Review your questions just prior to the interview; then put them away.

OBSERVATIONS

Try very diligently to attend any meetings on the subject of interviewing which may be conducted by the placement office, faculty, Accounting Club or Beta Alpha Psi. The pointers you pick up may be ones you are already aware of (i.e., polish your shoes, clean fingernails, etc.), but they are all important. If asked, several firms may even be willing to conduct live mock interviews in front of your organization. Other firms have video tapes of interviews that will give you additional pointers. Avail yourself of all these to better prepare yourself.

NUMBER OF INTERVIEWS

Most students interested in a public accounting career interview between six and ten firms. Although no accurate statistics are available, it appears that the average student interviews with approximately eight firms—most of the Big 8, then Non-Big 8, national and local firms.

The number you interview with is immaterial. What is important is the number of invitations you receive to visit offices. Some students are reluctant to let a firm know that

they are interviewing with or have received invitations or
even offers from other firms. This secrecy is not necessary
or recommended. Let it be known far and wide that others
are interested in you. But also be coy enough to let it be
known that, while many are interested in you, you have the
most interest in the firm you are speaking with at the moment.

Do not be cocky about your success. Sincere humility is
a strong virtue and will contribute to your success when
coupled with sincere interest in a firm.

On the other hand, if you have twenty interviews, keep
it a secret between yourself and your placement office. You
will be tagged as indecisive (because you cannot choose a
career) or as a loser who cannot get a job.

INTERVIEW TIMING

"Should I interview in the fall, winter or spring? In the
morning, mid-day or late afternoon?"

As soon as you return to campus from summer break,
you should check with your placement office to ascertain
which firms have scheduled fall interview dates. Most large
firms conduct campus interviews in October and schedule
office visits in November, December and January. Offers
of employment are extended and accepted during this timeframe even though starting dates may be scheduled for June
through September. If you send your resume, many firms
will also agree to a screening interview in their office during
the summer before you return to campus. This courtesy is
especially applicable to students who attend colleges where
the firm does not schedule on-campus interviewing dates.
There is nothing wrong with accepting a position that has a
June or July starting date as early as the prior December or
January. Think of all the freedom that will result during
your last term! Also, consider that CPA firms are very busy
with year-end audits and tax return preparation during the
winter; but throughout the fall more staff are available to
see you during your office visit. This will give you a better
picture of the office and its staff.

As to the best time of day to interview, you will get vastly differing opinions from almost everyone. However, most agree that the first interview and the last are worst. If your interview is the first of the day, beware that the interviewer may not yet have had a second cup of coffee and, if you're scheduled last, know that he may be anxious to leave. The first interview after lunch may not be too good either. Many interviewers lunch with faculty and return late. These interviewers will try to catch up with their schedules, which may mean that they will not give you the benefit of a full half-hour. There is no consensus in this matter, but most believe that the third and fourth interview slots of the day are best. The interviewer is awake, has had some coffee and is not yet tired.

Also, consider positioning your interview immediately after several students who you believe will be rejected. If you are as good as you think you are, you may look even better in comparison with several weaker students.

If you are really good, the time of your interview does not matter.

PRACTICE

Practice interviewing! Need more be said? Find a friend and interview each other. It is better to stutter, stumble and make your mistakes before your first interview than to become polished during your fourth interview after three rejections based on your nerves. Remember, you want to persuade the interviewer of the value you bring to that firm if hired. It is virtually impossible to do that if you are so "psyched out" by the interview format that you are unable to string five words into a coherent sentence. By practicing, you can greatly reduce or eliminate the fear of the unknown. If you cannot find a friend, use a mirror. You may find that you are your own best critic, but PRACTICE!

SUMMARY

Your interview goals are:

> P repare
> R eceive office invitations
> E mployment offers
> P osition acceptance

PREParation is one of the most important components of your interview. Interviewers do not expect you to learn in an interview. They expect you to know what you want *PRIOR* to the interview and to use the interview to evaluate the firm. Do your homework before your interviews.

3 CAMPUS INTERVIEW

There are four main reasons for campus interviews—three for the firm and one for the student. The firm's reasons are:

- to evaluate students to be selected for an office visit,
- to develop interest in the firm, and
- to build goodwill with all students.

The student's primary reason is to receive an invitation to visit the office.

FIRM'S REASONS

TO EVALUATE STUDENTS TO BE SELECTED FOR AN OFFICE VISIT. When students think of a campus interview, they usually think of the evaluative portion of the interview—that short portion of the thirty minutes when they are asked questions about their past, present and future. This is usually the most feared portion of an interview because you feel you must "sell" yourself or divulge information which you may prefer to keep secret.

The words on this page will not overcome your nervousness, but let me emphasize that this is the easiest portion of the interview—if you have prepared and know what to expect. After all, you know yourself better than anyone. The interviewer probably knows nothing about you. Therefore, the story you tell and the way you present it will form the basis upon which the interviewer will make a decision. Preparation and practice before the interview are a must.

TO DEVELOP AN INTEREST IN THE FIRM. In addition to evaluating you, the interviewer is charged with the responsibility of *SELLING THE FIRM TO YOU.* Generally, in response to your question, the interviewer will describe positive differences between firms, highlight strengths, define programs and policies or, in general, attempt to sell you on the virtues of beginning your career at his firm.

TO BUILD GOODWILL WITH ALL STUDENTS. A good interviewer "leaves 'em all smiling." Whether you are invited into the office or rejected, you will probably be someone, somewhere, someday; so the interviewer will not want to turn you off or offend you in any way. You will probably leave the interview with a good feeling. Hopefully, you will tell your friends what a great interview you had or how impressed you were with "X" firm.

STUDENT'S REASON

TO RECEIVE AN INVITATION TO VISIT THE OFFICE. From a student's standpoint there is only one reason for a campus interview: *Receive an invitation to visit the office.* Place this statement firmly in your mind. If you do not receive an office visit as a result of your campus interviews, everything is for naught: career plans, four years of college in preparation for a career, dreams, desires, lifestyle, etc.

Having a great interview, being excited about a firm or receiving the right answers to your questions are all wasted if you do not receive an invitation.

Your goal must remain the same for each interview. Since you may not receive an offer from every office visit, you must continually strive during each campus interview to receive additional office visits. This not only improves your odds at receiving an offer but increases your chances for multiple offers. With only one offer, you do not have a choice. You will probably accept that offer. And therefore the decision on your employer was really made for you, not by you. However, if you receive several offers, you are in the driver's seat and can choose the best offer.

Of course, you should also use your interview to learn about the firm.

IMPORTANCE

Now that you know the reasons for a campus interview, let's put them into perspective. How important is each of your interviews? There is widespread belief that your interview is *the most important half-hour of your life.* Out of the interview process you make a decision affecting the rest of your life.

- Assuming you spend your career with the firm you begin with, you will spend more waking hours with that firm than with your family—100,000 hours—by working only 2,300 hours per year over a 44 year career.

- You are making what could potentially be a multi-million-dollar decision. Career earnings in some firms have been estimated as high as $8,000,000. (Compute an annual average of $60,000 compounded and inflated over 45 years. Then realize that the average Big-8 partner is already earning more than $180,000 a year.)

DETERMINING HIRING QUOTAS

Before we get into the interview itself, let's look at how a firm determines the number of students to be invited for office visits.

Through whatever manpower planning techniques an office employs, the number of new hires is predetermined. The predetermined number of new staff will affect the number of office visits to extend and the number of offers to be made. For example:

> Firm ABC will hire 20 new graduates this year. If we assume that only 50 percent of those who receive offers will accept those offers (acceptance rate), the ABC firm must make offers of employment to 40 graduates.

> If only 75 percent of those invited to the office receive offers, then the ABC firm will have to invite 53 students into the office.

> So if ABC wants 20 new staff members, they will have to plan on 53 office visits.

Acceptance rates, however, vary among firms and individual offices. Some may be as low as 25 percent and others as high as 75 percent. Most fall in the 40 to 50 percent range and are relatively constant from year to year in each office.

MODEL CAMPUS INTERVIEW

The typical campus interview is divided into several phases. What follows is a model interview. It is used in training interviewers for most accounting firms, and is the type interview you will encounter most frequently. The amount of time devoted to each phase will vary from interview to interview, but the basic structure will remain intact.

Your interview will last thirty minutes and the "interview clock" should look like this:

INTERVIEWER

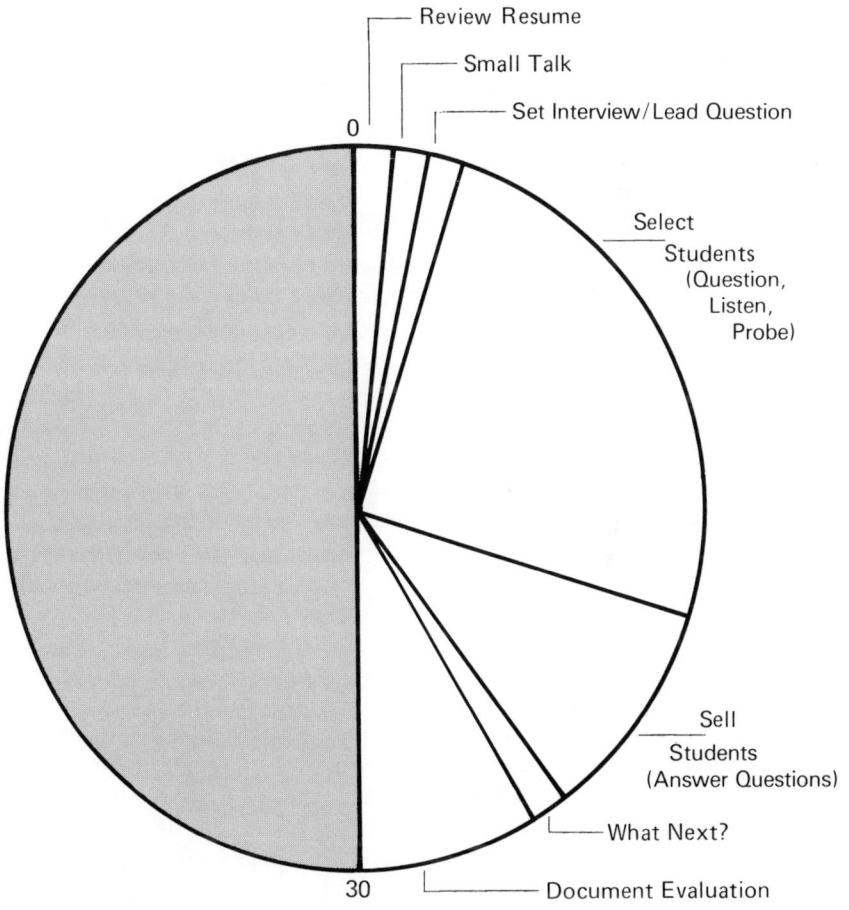

Review Resume

Small Talk

Set Interview/Lead Question

0

Select
Students
(Question,
Listen,
Probe)

Sell
Students
(Answer Questions)

What Next?

30

Document Evaluation

41

MODEL CAMPUS INTERVIEW

Interviewer	Time Elapsed (in minutes)	Student
Review Resume and Meet Student		
Scans resume to become familiar with salient points (i.e., classroom and job experience, extracurricular activities, interests, etc.) and meets student. (1 minute)	1	Wipes sweaty palms for the last time, takes a deep breath and may even say a little prayer. *Handshake with the interviewer is very important; make it firm and business-like. Smile! Call the interviewer by surname (Mr., Mrs.) unless asked to use a first name.*
Small Talk		
Engages in small talk with student of a non-stressful nature (i.e., weather, a common interest, an interesting point or event on a student's resume or credentials or interview results). (1 minute)	2	Establishes eye contact. Stands until the interviewer sits down. Adjusts his chair before being seated. *The interviewer is not your enemy. He or she is paid to select qualified candidates. If you project your-self as qualified, whether you are or not, you have a good chance at receiving an office invitation. Do not be yourself.*

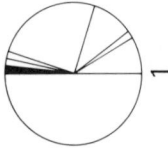

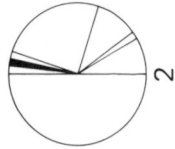

Interviewer	Time Elapsed (in minutes)	Student
Set Interview/Lead Question		
Outlines an agenda for interview; sets stage (i.e., "I'll ask you some questions, then give you an opportunity to ask questions concerning our firm. I would like to begin with: why, when, how, etc. . . .") (1 minute)	3	Agrees, smiles, appears anxious and interested. *The impression you have created so far may well set the tone for the remainder of the interview.*
Select Students		
Uses information provided on resume to draw out additional information regarding classroom and job experiences, extracurricular activities and interests so as to determine behavioral patterns and motivations. Most interviewers like to begin with a "broad-brush" question and follow-up questions requiring you to give more than a one-word answer. (16 minutes)	19	Answers questions in a conversational manner. *This is the "interview" feared by some. The way you answer questions is as important as the answers themselves. Enthusiasm, interest, excitement, even a sparkle in your eye (corny, but true) are very important. Depending on the interviewer, you may encounter anything from an easygoing, smooth conversation to stress (you're really on the hot seat).*

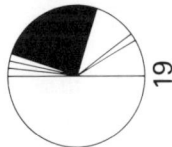

continued

Interviewer	Time Elapsed (in minutes)	Student
Sell Students		You are now the interviewer. Ask questions! *Many students are still "alive" up to this point, but stumble on the question, "Now what can I tell you about our firm?" Be prepared to demonstrate that you not only have a good knowledge of the profession, firm and career, but also that you have a genuine interest in acquiring particular information of concern to you (review questions later in this chapter).*
Gives clear, concise and positive answers to student's questions. (5 minutes)		
	24	
What Next?		Expect to be told about further contact. Ask if necessary. State that you are impressed by the firm, interview or interviewer (something) and that you certainly hope for a favorable response. End the interview by standing, shaking hands, thanking the interviewer and leave smiling.
Tells student what to expect next: "You'll hear from us in writing within two weeks. Nice meeting you, see you soon." (1 minute)		
	25	

44

Interviewer	Time Elapsed (in minutes)	Student
Document Evaluation Makes a decision to invite, reject or refer the student to another office and then documents his decision on an evaluation form (see pages 62-65 for sample forms). (5 minutes)	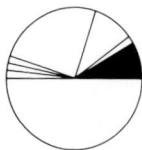 30	Reflects on the past 25 minutes and what he has learned that can help him with his next interview.

CAMPUS INTERVIEW
WHAT REALLY HAPPENS

REVIEW RESUME AND MEET STUDENT

At this moment your career rests on a piece of paper. It must be neat and present you in a positive light. A smile, a firm handshake (ladies too) and the use of surnames are important. From the moment the interviewer first sees you, you are being evaluated. Impressions formed during previous meetings (Beta Alpha Psi banquets, etc.) are also being confirmed or reassessed. Sit in your chair at the same time or after the interviewer sits. Move your chair slightly before sitting down to give the impression of "taking charge." It is better to lean forward in your chair than to sit back and totally relax. (There is a story of an experienced interviewer who intentionally slouched in his chair to the point that the student followed suit and slid out of his chair.) Your every move is being judged and evaluated. Additionally, some interviewers attempt to make their decision within the first five minutes of an interview. Be on your best behavior, and on guard. *DO NOT BE YOURSELF. BE WHAT THE INTERVIEWER WANTS YOU TO BE—A BUSINESSPERSON.* (Be yourself when you are deciding which offer to ac-

SMALL TALK

The interviewer knows or at least assumes you may be nervous. A good interviewer will attempt to help you by engaging in small talk about something you should be able to talk about with no fear—the weather, an interesting point on your resume, a common interest, sports, your interviews, etc. Take advantage of this opportunity to "relax into" your interview "character"—the person you want the interviewer to think you are.

Caution: acting or not being yourself in an interview requires much planning and practice. Without practice you will surely do yourself a lot of harm. Acting in this drama is not for amateurs. Practice and play the role of a businessperson who brings significant value to the firm that hires you.

SET INTERVIEW

Many interviewers will not outline the remainder of the 30 minutes for you. They assume you know what to expect.

SELECT STUDENT:
QUESTIONS YOU WILL BE ASKED

Most interviewers have two or three standard questions they ask students. Some firms require that one or two questions be asked during each interview. However, most questions asked during an interview are developed during the interview itself as part of a conversation and are designed to allow the interviewer to assess apparent strengths/weaknesses and identify additional information needs beyond the resume facts.

Questions will probably be asked of you by the interviewer in some or all of the following areas: classroom experiences, job experiences, extracurricular activities and personal interests. You will also be evaluated on your personal behavior during the interview and at all other meetings with the interviewer or other firm representative.

In the area of *CLASSROOM EXPERIENCES* the interviewer may want to know about: grades, courses taken, professors, electives taken, number of hours per term, special projects, pass/fail courses, faculty recommendations, papers or publications, courses related to accounting, number of hours spent studying and more.

- What is your GPA?
- What is your accounting GPA?
- What was your GPA for the first two years vs. last year?
- What courses did you enjoy most? Least?
- What professors did you enjoy most? Least?
- In what course did you learn the most? Least? Why?
- Why did you choose accounting as a major?
- How, why or when did you choose public accounting?

- What courses have you completed?
- Which courses do you have remaining?
- What electives have you taken? Why?
- How many hours did you carry per term?
- Why did you decide to attend ABC University?
- What research projects have you been involved with?
- Does your GPA reflect your knowledge of accounting/business? Why?
- How have you utilized technology to resolve problems?
- Why did you take XXX course as pass/fail?
- What kind of recommendation will I get from Dr. XXX?
- What is your class standing?
- What were your SAT scores? PSAT? LSAT, etc.?
- Others?

In the area of *JOB EXPERIENCES* the interviewer may want to know about: percent of college expenses earned, types of jobs, how you obtained the jobs, relevancy to accounting, number of jobs, duration of job, hours per week, supervisory experiences, accomplishments, advancement, responsibilities and more.

- What did you do on this job?
- What did you learn from this experience?
- How did you get the job?
- What were your responsibilities?
- How do you feel you enhanced the job?
- How did you get along with your boss? Peers?
- How were you treated?
- Did you enjoy the work?
- If you had your boss's job, what would you do differently?
- Do you consider yourself an entrepreneur? Why?
- Have you ever supervised others? What did you learn?
- Do you consider this job as a learning experience or as a "pay the rent" job? Why?

- Which do you like better: challenging or routine work? Why?
- How many hours did you work per week?
- Why did you leave this job?
- What kind of reference will I get?
- What special skills have you developed?
- How much of your college expenses did you earn? Loans? Grants? Scholarships?
- What did you learn that you could apply to your career?
- Others?

In the area of *EXTRACURRICULAR ACTIVITIES* the interviewer may want to know about: level of participation, responsibilities accepted, achievements, roles or positions, circle of influence or friends, elective offices held, programs initiated, speaking experiences and more.

- What organizations do you belong to? Why?
- How active are you?
- Did you have any leadership roles? How obtained? Responsibilities? Duties?
- Who are your closest friends?
- How have you improved your organization?
- How much time do you devote?
- When you begin your career, what organizations would you like to join?
- Tell me about . . . ?
- In what community activities have you been involved? How did you happen to select those?
- Which do you like better: spectator or participant activities? Why?
- Others?

In the area of *PERSONAL INTERESTS* the interviewer may want to know about: participative and spectator activities, interests, difficulty of interests, motivators and challengers, time involvement, ability, communication skills and personal demeanor, hobbies and more.

- What are your hobbies and interests? Why? Most enjoyed?

- How do you prioritize your activities?
- What does your family think about your chosen profession?
- How do you stay abreast of general business issues outside the classroom?
- What have you learned from them? How?
- What turns you on?
- What turns you off?
- How would you rate yourself as a public speaker?
- How do you rate your writing skills?
- Do you want to work in my firm? Why?
- Why are you interested in us?
- Which firm or firms do you like best so far? Why?
- How much do you expect to earn your first year? Fifth year?
- In what city do you want to work? Why?
- Are you willing to travel? Work overtime?
- Others?

You will also be evaluated during the interview on *PERSONAL BEHAVIOR*. The interviewer will be looking for such things as: dress, appearance, grooming, posture, body language, eye contact, enthusiasm, interest, alertness, communication skills, positive motivation, mannerisms, questions, self-confidence, assertiveness, aggressiveness, poise, tact, maturity, business sense and more; or in other words, a person with a well-rounded personality, maturity and a genuine desire to achieve in business.

With the above five areas in mind, you should now develop additional questions that could be asked of you during the interview. If you take the time to develop the questions now, you will not only be aware of most questions that could be asked in an interview, but you will almost automatically have developed answers for each of your questions. Try the questions and answers out on a friend or a mirror. Speaking aloud will help you to develop not only the right answers but also a convincing delivery. A tape recorder may also assist you. This level of preparation is important, but do not allow yourself to fall into the trap of rote memorization. Your delivery must be fresh and sincere, in spite of answering the same question for 10 different interviewers.

Now let's ask a few of those standard questions you can expect to be asked.

Tell me about yourself! This question (actually a statement) has started more interviews than any other. It is both a stress question (can you talk for 30 minutes or not?) and a bad place to begin an interview. A good candidate will probably smile and ask the interviewer where to begin. What has the interviewer gained? Nothing!

Personal feelings aside on the quality of this question, you will no doubt start several interviews this way. Some interviewers still like the question because they believe it will give some insight into your motivations, drives and accomplishments (i.e., where you begin, what you choose to mention, your delivery, etc.).

Prepare a 30 second to one minute speech about yourself. For example: "I was born and raised in . . . I attended Austin High School where I lettered in track and was treasurer of my Junior Class. I believe it was this exposure as treasurer that led me to major in accounting. Before I graduated from Austin, I decided to major in accounting in college. Because my grades were 3.6 at Austin, I was accepted at all five colleges where I had applied. But I chose to come here to . . . University because of the reputation of the accounting program and faculty. While here at . . . University, I have maintained a 3.2 overall and a 3.4 GPA in accounting. I believe a balance between academics and social life is important. Therefore, I joined a social fraternity where I am rush chairman and Beta Alpha Psi where I am again a treasurer. Incidentally, as you can see on my resume, I've worked construction jobs each summer to earn 60 percent of my college expenses and have been a grader for Dr. Jones' 301 class for about 15 hours per week during the last two terms. When I have a few spare minutes from studies and the fraternities, I like to jog, swim and play golf. Now, could I fill you in on any of the details?"

What have you done in the last . . . (any length of time)

that you are most gratified with? This question is a motivation probe. What turns you on? There is no set answer to
the question. The way you answer (clearly, with conciseness
and logic, using good communication skills) is as important
to the answer as the event itself. The event should be an ac-
complishment directed by you and confirmed by others for
the good of all (motherhood and apple pie). For example:
"I was the most gratified when, after being elected treasurer
of my fraternity, I used skills which I had learned in the
classroom to finally balance our budget."

What do you expect to be doing in 5, 10, and 20 years?
This is also a motivational probe. It gives the student an opportunity to show preparedness for the interview or to dig a
hole which is difficult or impossible to climb out of. Having
done your homework, you know that in 5 years you will
probably be a manager or close to it, close to partner in 10
years and a well-paid partner in 20 years. (Perhaps a managing partner, National Industry Specialist partner, etc.) State
these facts to show you're prepared. Overstating tends to be
pompous and understating shows either a lack of assertiveness or ignorance. The wrong answer is "I don't
know," "I'm not sure" or to infer in any way that your
goals are anything except partnership in the firm you are
talking with. You may be asked "What do you know about
being a partner?" If you have done your homework, you
will know that a partner is expected to: provide clients with
quality service and serve as a business advisor, bring new
business into the firm, develop managers and staff, and
maintain leadership visibility in professional and community organizations. In short, they are faster than a speeding
bullet and jump tall buildings in a single bound! To say that
you intend on having your own practice someday may show
aggressiveness, but "your own practice" is plainly not the
firm which your interviewer represents.

How are your interviews going? Many interviewers like
this question, or variations of it, and use it frequently. A
wealth of information can be gained by the interviewer, and
the student has an excellent opportunity to sell himself. The
firm will obtain information from your answers:

- What other interviewers think of you.
- Your interest in public accounting.
- Your ability to speak effectively.
- Your interview successes and failures.
- Which firm(s) you like best/least and why.

Students have an opportunity to:

- Sell themselves to the interviewer.
- Speak on a subject of common interest to which only you know the answers.
- Express interest in public accounting in general and the firm in particular.

Prepare your answer, as this could be one of the first questions asked. Possible answers are:

- This is my first interview.
- This is my first of eight interviews.
- This is my seventh interview. I have received office visit invitations from three and have yet to hear from the remaining interviews of last week.
- This is my fourth campus interview. I'm really excited about the prospect of a public accounting career and have been looking forward to interviewing with your firm. (Be prepared for a "Why?" to this answer. You really did not tell the interviewer anything, so there will be further probing.)

All of the above represent positive statements; you are selling yourself! Please do not let negative "vibes" enter into answers such as:

- I began interviewing five weeks ago and have not yet heard from anyone. (You will usually hear from firms within two weeks and interviewers know it, or know which firms may happen to be slow. All firms will not be slow.)
- "This is my fourth interview. I've received three rejections and one invitation." True statement perhaps, but negative! Better to have said "I have had four interviews and have received one invita-

tion.'' This is also a true statement but said in a positive, salesman-like manner. If the interviewer wants to know about your rejections, if any, let him or her ask.

Never tell a lie; it will eventually catch up with you and impact negatively. Develop an answer before your interview and practice it in a businesslike, humble and positive way.

"STUPID QUESTIONS"

There is an old adage that "the only stupid question was the one that was never asked." This is not necessarily true in some interview situations. While most interviewers are trained in proper questioning techniques, chances are good that you will at some point encounter an interviewer who asks certain questions which seem irrelevant or even ridiculous. These interviewers are generally not trying to intimidate you, but their lack of training in asking these questions may result in doing just that. The questions are usually hypothetical ("What if . . .") in nature and there is no right or wrong answer. Examples are:

"What if we were at your funeral. What do you think your friends and family would be saying about you?"

"If you had three wishes, what would you wish for?"

"If you could be a movie star, famous comedian or professional athlete, which would you choose and why?"

It is doubtful that most students have ever thought about the answers to these questions, which is exactly what the interviewer is counting on to ensure an "unrehearsed" response. His objective? To gain a glimpse into your "inner self."

As previously mentioned, there are no right or wrong answers to questions of this nature. Part of your preparation is in knowing that these questions may be asked. Another tip is to PAUSE before answering. Reflect on the question and don't rush your answer. This gives you time to digest what the interviewer might interpret from your response. Always remember that interviewers are looking for future business leaders who are intuitive, decisive, team players able to think on their feet and resolve problems. Your specific answer is less important than how you handle the question. If you jump right in and ramble endlessly while at the same time trying to digest the question, it is virtually impossible to demonstrate a professional demeanor ("executive presence"). The qualities you believe you possess to be successful in the professional world will be inherent in your answer if you have accurately assessed the question.

With this in mind, let's "walk through" a potential response to the first question noted above and the reaction an interviewer might have as he hears it:

(PAUSE TO DIGEST QUESTION AND FORMULATE RESPONSE) "I am very close to my family and have a number of close friends (family values, pleasant personality, probable team player). While the thought of dying is not something I have ever dwelled upon (you are probably not a negative person or pessimist), I suspect their words would reflect great sorrow. You see, they know me as a goal oriented person who expects to accomplish much during my lifetime (you plan to work hard and be successful). To be denied that opportunity would be very tragic in their minds . . . and as you might expect, the thought doesn't exactly make me want to dance in the streets either!" (Interviewer appreciates humor—you handled it well.)

ILLEGAL QUESTIONS

Demographics of the average college graduate have changed dramatically. There are more "non-traditional" students than five or ten years ago. These include individuals who are married, have children, or are much older than the "typical" student. In many cases, this type of business student may have spent time in another career (teaching, working in a factory, etc.) or raised a family before going to college for an accounting degree.

You should be aware that there are Federal, State and in some cases, local laws which prohibit interviewers from asking questions and basing employment decisions on age, sex, marital status, race, religious affiliation, whether you have children, or basically any area which has no bearing on your qualifications to do the job. Except for the hypothetical questions previously discussed, an interviewer can only ask (legally) about work experience, academic record, extracurricular activities and personal interests (hobbies, etc.).

If you are asked an illegal question, it is up to you whether or not to respond. You may wish to diplomatically state "I am happy to answer that question but first, would you mind telling me how it is relevant to my qualifications for a position with your firm?" Some students have reported success with "turning the tables" such as "how does being married affect *your* (or your partners') ability to do the job?"

Obviously, there is no easy way to deal with these types of questions. There is always the risk of offending the interviewer and being rejected. You must ask yourself, "do I really *want* to work for a firm that bases hiring (and maybe promotions) on criteria other than ability?" Incidentally, be sure to inform your placement office and faculty if you are asked illegal questions. Most schools have procedures in place to prohibit campus recruiting by specific interviewers or entire firms if they practice illegal interviewing tactics.

Why? The word "why" beginning any question is a low-key threat, or a word that can be stressful ("Why did you choose _____?"). Most interviewers do not mean to create stress by the use of "why" but will use it to determine your behavior.

SELL-STUDENT— QUESTIONS YOU SHOULD ASK

As mentioned, you must be prepared to ask the interviewer questions for several reasons:

- to gather information about the firm
- to demonstrate your interest in the firm, and
- to keep the interviewer talking to fill the half hour.

Preview Chapter 4 at this point to determine how to ask questions. *YOU* are now the interviewer.

This is also an opportunity to display the quality of your research on the firm to the interviewer. Begin each question with a fact that you have determined from your conversations with faculty, the placement office, recent graduates working for the firm or materials you have read (Wall Street Journal, Public Accounting Report, Big 8 Review, Accounting Today, Journal of Accountancy or Firm Brochures). Some examples:

> "I understand you recently introduced into the market a new audit software package called XXX. What experience might I have using this software during my first year? What other technological advances do you see coming that will affect the profession?"

> or,

> "In speaking with John Doe who joined your firm last year, I learned that your entry level staff training includes a discussion of the firm's audit approach, utilization of microcomputers and even role-playing on interviewing clients. What else can I expect at this course as well as additional training during my career?

Do not ask questions simply to take up time. You should be sincerely interested in the subject area. Our point is that the competition for quality positions is intense, and you can greatly enhance your chance for success if you utilize appropriate research resources and let your interviewer know you are *very serious* about an opportunity with his firm.

To stimulate your thinking and provide you with a starting point, below are a few questions on common topics asked properly and improperly. Please take the time to develop additional questions (and answers) concerning your wants, needs and desires.

PROPER	IMPROPER
I've read your brochure and see that you have a training program. Could you tell me more about the first-year training, or specialized courses, etc.?	Do you have a training program?
How many client assignments might I expect in the first year? How would these assignments be determined?	Will I be stuck on one client?
Do not ask about salary or benefits during a campus interview. Only ask— if not told prior—after you receive an offer.	What fringe benefits do you have?
I expect travel and overtime. Could you explain how much I might expect in your office?	How much overtime will I work or how much will I be expected to travel?
All firms have developed quality control programs, but the brochure only mentioned that yours is excellent. Could you explain more about yours?	Do you have a quality control program?
Dr. Smith of our faculty mentioned several of your clients. Could you give me a breakdown of your clients and their industry groups?	Who are your clients?
How many professionals are on your staff and in what departments are they?	How big is your office?
I expect to begin on the audit staff but may like to specialize in taxes someday. Is that possible in your office now or in the future?	Can I get into taxes and consulting?
What can you tell me that will differentiate your firm from the others?	Why should I work for your firm?
I talked to John ____ who interned with you last summer. He said he worked on two municipal audits. Could you tell me more about your municipal practice?	Is your practice heavy in municipal audits?

58

PROPER	IMPROPER
I want to pass the CPA Exam as quickly as possible. What is the average number of sittings for your current staff and how will you help me pass?	How long do I have to pass the CPA Exam?
In what type of civic, social, and community activities would your firm encourage me to be active?	Am I encouraged to be active in community activities?
Many firms have been in trouble with the SEC. Would you please explain your record to me?	I heard your firm was in trouble with the SEC. What happened?
What else can I tell you about myself that will help me get onto your staff? Frankly I want to.	Are we finished?

Develop your own questions below. You may want to preview the Decision Matrix in Chapter 6 to assist in developing questions concerning your wants, needs and desires.

PROPER	IMPROPER
	(None please)

Do not feel that every question you develop must be asked (the "shopping list" approach). Develop your series of questions and be prepared to go off into any direction the conversation may take. Remember you are the interviewer and should employ not only good questioning techniques, but also good listening techniques as described in Chapter 4. Your interest displayed by several good questions and the body language employed while listening are more important than a barrel full of poorly asked questions.

WHAT NEXT?

Make sure that you know when you leave your interview how and when you will be contacted by the firm. You can ask the interviewer for a business card.

DOCUMENT EVALUATION

The interviewer will evaluate you on some type of evaluation form. Several samples appear on the following pages. Notice that a decision is made on every form to invite, reject or refer you.

EVALUATION FORMS

Several firms have given their consent to reproduce copies of their Campus Interview Evaluation form for your benefit. Study these forms and you will realize what firms are looking for.

COOPERS & LYBRAND

CANDIDATE RECORD

NAP 100 (10/77)

CANDIDATE NUMBER	NAME (LAST NAME FIRST)		COLLEGE NAME	COLLEGE CODE

I   **O**   320

(1-7)   (8-27)   (28-30)

INTERVIEWER NUMBER

O

(33-40)

INTERVIEWER NAME

SOURCE(41)	RACE (42)	SEX (43)	DEGREE (53)	AVERAGE (A = 4.0)	CLASS STANDING (58-59)
Campus ☐C	White ☐W	Male ☐M	Bachelors ☐B	Overall (54-55)	Top 10% ☐10
Walk-In ☐W	Black ☐B	Female ☐F	Masters ☐M		Top 25% ☐25
Intern ☐I	Asian ☐A	Init.	Law ☐L		Top Half ☐50
Agency ☐A	Hispanic ☐H	Cont.	Major:	Acctg (56-57)	Bottom Half ☐75
	Am. Indian ☐I	Date (46-51)			

CAMPUS INTERVIEW EVALUATIONS

MOTIVATION

UNACCEPTABLE ☐   SATISFACTORY ☐   GOOD ☐   OUTSTANDING ☐

(POSITIVE, ENERGETIC, MOTIVATED, SUCCESSFUL, GOAL-ORIENTED, ENTHUSIASTIC)
COMMENTS:

COMMUNICATIONS SKILLS

UNACCEPTABLE ☐   SATISFACTORY ☐   GOOD ☐   OUTSTANDING ☐

(ARTICULATE, LISTENS, POISED, TACTFUL, CONVINCING)
COMMENTS:

EXECUTIVE PRESENCE

UNACCEPTABLE ☐   SATISFACTORY ☐   GOOD ☐   OUTSTANDING ☐

(IMPRESSIVE, LEVELHEADED, AT EASE, AWARE, SELF-CONFIDENT)
COMMENTS:

INTELLECTUAL ABILITIES

UNACCEPTABLE ☐   SATISFACTORY ☐   GOOD ☐   OUTSTANDING ☐

(INSIGHTFUL, CREATIVE, CURIOUS, IMAGINATIVE, UNDERSTANDS, REASONS, INTELLIGENT, SCHOLARLY)
COMMENTS:

JUDGMENT – DECISION-MAKING ABILITY

UNACCEPTABLE ☐   SATISFACTORY ☐   GOOD ☐   OUTSTANDING ☐

(MATURE, SEASONED, INDEPENDENT, COMMON SENSE, CERTAIN, LOGICAL)
COMMENTS:

LEADERSHIP

UNACCEPTABLE ☐   SATISFACTORY ☐   GOOD ☐   OUTSTANDING ☐

(SELF-CONFIDENT, TAKES CHARGE, DETERMINED, EFFECTIVE, RESPECTED, MANAGEMENT MINDED, GRASPS AUTHORITY)
COMMENTS:

CAMPUS INTERVIEW SUMMARY

INVITE (Circle)	AREA OF INTEREST (Circle)	SEMESTER HRS.	OFFICES PREFERRED:	SUMMARY COMMENTS:
YES NO	AUDIT TAX	Acct'g.	No. 1	
DATE AVAILABLE	MCS ABC	Audit	No. 2	
	Other	Tax	No. 3	

OVERALL EVALUATION (60)	DATE INVITED TO C&L OFFICE	INITIAL RECV'G OFFICE		SEND FORM TO NATIONAL RECRUITING WITHIN ONE WEEK OF CAMPUS VISIT.
Outstanding ☐O			A 2	NOTE: Referrals only — Send remainder of this form to receiving office
Good ☐G				along with candidate's resume; bcc receiving office on invitation
Average ☐A	(61-66)	(67-69)	(79-80)	letter.
Poor ☐P				

Reprinted with permission of Coopers & Lybrand

INTERVIEW EVALUATION

L‖H

Laventhol & Horwath

(attach resume)

NAME _____ INTERVIEW: FIRST ☐ SECOND ☐

POSITION _____ LOCATION PREFERENCE: FIRST _____ SECOND _____

CANDIDATE CONTENT REMARKS (Content — related to job duties and responsibilities) _____

CANDIDATE CONTEXT REMARKS (Context — environmental factors) _____

LEADERSHIP, INTELLECTUAL ABILITIES OUTSTANDING ☐ DESIRABLE ☐ AVERAGE ☐ QUESTIONABLE ☐ UNSUITABLE ☐
(Self-confident, effective, sincere, creative, diplomatic, imaginative, incisive)

ATTITUDE, MOTIVATION, GOALS OUTSTANDING ☐ DESIRABLE ☐ AVERAGE ☐ QUESTIONABLE ☐ UNSUITABLE ☐
(Energetic, alert, goal oriented, self-Starter, positive, ambitious, dynamic)

JUDGEMENT, MATURITY OUTSTANDING ☐ DESIRABLE ☐ AVERAGE ☐ QUESTIONABLE ☐ UNSUITABLE ☐
(Independent, keen, logical, levelheaded, aware, perceptive)

COMMUNICATION SKILLS OUTSTANDING ☐ DESIRABLE ☐ AVERAGE ☐ QUESTIONABLE ☐ UNSUITABLE ☐
(Articulate, persuasiveness, enthusiastic, clarity, tactful)

PRESENCE OUTSTANDING ☐ DESIRABLE ☐ AVERAGE ☐ QUESTIONABLE ☐ UNSUITABLE ☐
(Grooming, poise, appearance)

OVERALL RATING OF POTENTIAL	OUTSTANDING Should Invite or Refer*	DESIRABLE May Invite or Refer*	UNSUITABLE Reject

DISPOSITION: REJECT ☐ INVITE BACK TO OFFICE ☐ REFER TO _____ OFFICE ☐

REMARKS: _____

INTERVIEWER _____ DATE: _____

P-002   *(Complete I, II, III on reverse)   9/77

Reprinted with permission of Laventhol & Horwath (Front)

63

I. SPECIAL INTERESTS _____

II. SUGGESTIONS FOR OFFICE VISIT _____

III. REASON FOR OFFICE PREFERRED (REFERRAL)_____

IV. OTHER COMMENTS OR NOTES _____
_____
_____
_____

TELEPHONE REFERENCE CHECK

COMPANY	_____	_____
COMPANY REPRESENTATIVE	_____	_____
AND TITLE	_____	_____
DATES OF EMPLOYMENT	FROM_____ TO_____	FROM_____ TO_____
STARTING POSITION	_____	_____
STARTING SALARY	_____	_____
POSITION WHEN LEFT	_____	_____
DUTIES LAST POSITION	_____	_____
	_____	_____
	_____	_____
LAST SALARY WAS	_____	_____
RATE ABILITY AND WORK	_____	_____
ATTENDANCE RECORD:		
LATENESS	_____	_____
ABSENTEEISM	_____	_____
RELATIONSHIPS WITH OTHERS	_____	_____
REASON FOR LEAVING	_____	_____
WOULD YOU RE-HIRE	_____	_____
(EXPLAIN)	_____	_____
COMMENTS	_____	_____
	_____	_____
	_____	_____
REFERENCE CHECKED BY	_____	_____
DATE	_____	_____

Reprinted with permission of Laventhol & Horwath (Back)

64

INTERVIEWER'S APPRAISAL SHEET

SA SS SR	R L A H	R SI R O R A $	Date	1 2 3 4 5 6 7 8 9 10 11 12 13 14	Date

R - Raw
L - Light
A - Average
H - Heavy

R - Reject
SI - Second Interview
O - Offer
A - Acceptance

Numbers refer to S&S form letters in Recruiting Manual.

Applicant _____ Date _____

Position Applied For _____ Interviewer _____

(Check appropriate characteristics)	EXCELLENT	ACCEPTABLE	FAIR	POOR
GENERAL FIRST IMPRESSION				
PERSONAL APPEARANCE				
PERSONAL CHARACTERISTICS				
SCHOLASTIC RECORD				
WORK HISTORY				
TECHNICAL KNOWLEDGE APPEARS				
ABILITY OF EXPRESSION				
FINAL IMPRESSION				

PERSONALITY	EXPRESSION	POISE	MATURITY	CLERICAL EXPERIENCE
☐ Dominant	☐ Excellent	☐ Confident	☐ Exceptional	☐ Dictaphone
☐ Average	☐ Average	☐ Ordinary	☐ Normal	☐ Statistical
☐ Negative	☐ Evasive	☐ Nervous	☐ Insufficient	☐ File Room

Free and Willing to Travel _____ Yes _____ No   Saturday Availability _____ Yes _____ No

Health _____   Any independence problems? _____Yes _____No

EXPERIENCE

(a)	Writeups	_____	(k)	Stat. Samp.	_____	
(b)	Audits	_____	(l)	Brokerage	_____	
(c)	Out. Verif.	_____	(m)	Fiduciary	_____	
(d)	Inv. Observ.	_____	(n)	Real Estate	_____	
(e)	Report Prep.	_____	(o)	Typing WPM	_____	
(f)	Budgeting	_____	(p)	Mail Room	_____	
(g)	Costs	_____	(q)	Steno WPM	_____	
(h)	Data Proc.	_____	(r)	S'bd. Type	_____	
(i)	Tax Return Prep.	_____	(s)	Receptionist	_____	
(j)	Foreign Language	_____				

REMARKS

Adm. 9/30/79

1717-4

Reprinted with permission of Seidman & Seidman

INTERVIEW LOG

The moment you leave an interview you should take the time to record your thoughts, impressions and newfound knowledge for future reference. By the time you have had several interviews (campus and office visits), your thoughts and ideas will become vague and begin to run together. Therefore, please get in the habit of noting your impressions immediately after each campus interview and then completing your thoughts after your office visit.

A copy of a sample Interview Log is presented to help you organize your facts and opinions regarding each campus and office visit. Rather than printing ten copies of the Interview Log in this book, you should use the following example to develop your own log for each interview.

INTERVIEW LOG

Firm ....

Address ....

City, State, Zip ....

Phone (.......) ....

Interviewer-Campus ....

Interviewer-Office ....

Dates:

Campus Interview .... Time ....

Thank You Letter ....

Office Interview .... Time ....

Thank You Letter ....

Date Given for Decision ....

Notes:

Campus Interview: ....

....

....

....

....

Office Visit: ....

....

....

....

....

Offer $............................   Decision: Yes   No

FACE-TO-FACE REJECTION

An interviewer may decide during the campus interview that the student has no chance for an office visit. The interviewer may want to tell this to the student and surely the student should want to know. Unfortunately, however, nothing is usually said. The student must wait a week or two before learning that he has been rejected. Total honesty would be better for everyone during the interview but that, however, is not the pattern most interviews follow because interviewers are afraid of the potential negative backlash (i.e., a rejected student frequently thinks, "I'll fix that turkey for rejecting me," then tells all his friends what a lousy firm he interviewed with that afternoon.). The interviewer would prefer to have this reaction a week or two later—after other students have had a chance to form positive opinions about the firm.

SUMMARY

Now let's look at the interview as it really is. Your interviewer may be a full-time interviewer with the experience of thousands of interviews or a partner, manager or staff member on campus only one day. Regardless of the interviewer's experience, he will have some preconceived idea of what to look for—a "standard." In addition, the interviewer knows the number of students that can be invited to the office to satisfy the firm's needs.

In all likelihood the interviewer will speak to 12-15 students in a day. You are being compared to the other 11-14 students on the schedule and either rejected in the comparison to other students, or ranked—best to acceptable—among all acceptable students. At the end of the day or the next day in the office, the interviewer or interviewers will apply their standards to each of the students in relation to the number of office visits required. The decisions are made and invitation and rejection letters are sent.

The real point to be made is this: you are in competition with your peers and friends, so any advantage you can gain is to your benefit. This is where preparation pays huge dividends. For instance, if the interviewer knows you from a Beta Alpha Psi function, a faculty member has recommended you, you are a campus or club officer or leader, top in your class, etc., you have an almost unfair advantage over the unknown, untested student, or the one with a wet-fish handshake or no questions for the interviewer.

During a day of interviews, there will be extremes among students. A few students will clearly stand out as winners and may even receive a verbal invitation to visit the office during the campus interview. Most, however, will fail the campus interview for a myriad of reasons including poor interviewing skills. There are usually a few students on a schedule who fall in the middle—they are not clearly rejects nor are they clearly invites. These students are borderline for a number of reasons:

- Diamond in the rough,
- It's there, but he interviewed poorly,
- He interviews better than his credentials indicate he would,
- Is a little too shy,
- A bookworm,
- Poor grades but worked through school, etc.

These students may get a second and equal chance depending on the firm's needs.

You can increase the odds in your favor by being prepared. Interviewers have been overheard inviting students for an office visit on the way into the campus interview. Others have even been told to skip the campus interview and merely visit the office. Obviously, there is pre-interview contact. Who wins? The student and the firm! Who loses? All the unprepared students (reread Chapter 1)!

Back to the campus interview itself. You will answer questions and be expected to ask questions. Concerning questions you will be asked by the interviewer, turn to page 43 and place a "who," "what," "where," "when," "why" or "how" in front of each topic. This exercise will give you almost all the questions you will ever be asked. Seriously take the time to develop answers to each. Then say the answers aloud. How do they sound? Need more work? Once the answers sound good, try them out on a friend or in front of a mirror.

In regard to questions you will ask the interviewer, first preview Chapter 4 on questioning and listening techniques, then develop additional questions to ask. During this "sell" phase of an interview you must assume an interviewer's role and ask questions that will keep the firm's interviewer talking (selling the firm). Done skillfully, with open-ended questions, the interviewer will be selling not only a firm but also himself on you. In other words, you will accomplish your objective from the campus interview: *OBTAIN AN OFFICE VISIT.*

4 QUESTIONING AND LISTENING TECHNIQUES

QUESTIONING TECHNIQUES

Interviewers are trained to gather information beyond the facts presented in a student's credentials. Used properly these questions tend to create a free-flowing conversation, not one-word answers. Several types of questions are used:

BROAD-BRUSH
OPEN-ENDED
LEADING
PROBING

BROAD-BRUSH

A "broad-brush" question is a general question used to open an area of interest or general subject of conversation (i.e., "Could you tell me about your work experience or academic experiences or outside interests?"). A good "broad-brush" question is neither too broad (i.e., "Tell me

about yourself'') or too narrow (i.e., ''Did you like working
for ABC Company?'')

A student's ability to respond to this question will give
insight into motivation, creativity and communication
skills as well as ability to think on your own feet, as well as
provide the interviewer with additional information upon
which to probe further.

OPEN-ENDED

Like a broad-brush question, an open-ended question
cannot be answered by one word. It usually begins with
''who,'' ''what,'' ''where,'' ''why'' or ''how'' (i.e.,
''When did you decide on accounting as a career?'', ''Why
did you take systems?'', ''How did you do in Dr. Jones'
class?'').

LEADING QUESTION

The answer to a leading question is ''telegraphed'' to
the student before the question is asked. For instance:
''John, our business requires many hours of overtime. Are
you willing to work overtime?'' Be smart and give the
answer the interviewer is looking for: ''Yes, I'm willing to
work overtime.'' An even better response would be ''During the last three years I would guess that I work an average
of 20 hours per week overtime between my studies and job.
While it requires self discipline, I believe I am well prepared
for the overtime commitments required in the accounting
profession.''

PROBING

A probing question is a technique used to obtain information in a conversation which is in depth and meaningful.
Not to be considered interrogation, probing allows an interviewer to dig beyond bare facts. For example, a student
who says ''I'm secretary of my fraternity'' is only fur-
nishing a shallow statistic. Probing with ''what,'' ''where,''
''when,'' ''How active is the Chapter?'', ''How were you

elected?'' or ''Why did you run for office?'' will give the interviewer good evaluative information.

LISTENING TECHNIQUES

God gave interviewers two ears and one mouth. They are trained to use their faculties in that same ratio. Interviewers should listen more than they talk!

A trained interviewer will use the following listening techniques to encourage a student to continue talking:

MIRROR
SHOW ACCEPTANCE
SILENCE
BODY LANGUAGE
RESTATEMENT

MIRROR

Occasionally a student makes a statement which the interviewer wants expanded. The student may say, ''I really became involved in Beta Alpha Psi.'' The interviewer, wanting further information, just repeats part of the statement, ''Beta Alpha Psi'' encouraging the student to continue on the topic.

SHOW ACCEPTANCE

An interviewer encourages a student to continue talking by verbally acknowledging what has been said (i.e., ''I understand,'' ''I see,'' ''uh-huh,'' or ''okay'').

SILENCE

Five silent seconds in an interview seem like an eternity to any student, but that brief period is designed to keep the student talking. It can, however, destroy an unwary student because the interviewer will not fill the gap; it is up to the student to continue the conversation. Be careful not to ramble. Give whatever additional information is appropriate, then ask ''is there anything else you would like to know on that subject?''

BODY LANGUAGE

Forms of nonverbal communication such as eye contact, body and hand movement are used to keep a student talking and allow an interviewer to listen. Used in excess (staring, etc.) stress is introduced.

RESTATEMENT

An interviewer can pick out key statements from a dialogue and restate them in a way that will clarify or summarize. This will encourage additional input from the student.

SUMMARY

These questioning and listening techniques are taught to interviewers. Therefore it is important that students who want to be well-prepared learn and practice them. Used skillfully, the techniques will help you not only in your interviews but also in your entire business career.

5 OFFICE VISIT

PURPOSE

The purpose of this chapter is to:

- provide CPA firms about to begin a recruiting program with a guide and starting point from which to begin developing an effective and competitive office visit program; and
- provide students with an idea of what to expect during an office visit—especially the first.

OBJECTIVES

THE FIRM'S

From the firm's perspective, the objective of an office visit is to *SELL* itself to the student.

A secondary objective is to further evaluate the student. (Some estimates are that only 25-30% of the decision to extend an offer is made during the office visit, whereas 70-75% is made during the campus interview.) The campus interviewer (if effective) screened out students that would not likely receive an offer of employment. Therefore, the firm is generally predisposed to make an offer of employ-ment to those visiting the office, subject to their assessment of "fit" with the organization.

THE STUDENT'S

The student, of course, is trying to get an offer and is at the same time evaluating the firm, office and staff. *RECEIVING AN OFFER IS THE PRIME OBJECTIVE.*

Many students believe they will base their employment decision on the impressions drawn from the *PEOPLE* met during the office visit. This is a correct decision for the short-run only. Odds are that before a student becomes a partner in a firm, most if not all staff met during the visit will have left the firm. Also, the five or six staff met during the visit may or may not represent the office's overall per-sonality or all personalities in the office.

Therefore, while people are important to short-range decisions, there are more important decision points upon which to base a career. They are:
- the personality of the office, the managing partner and other partners,
- the philosophy of the firm and office with regard to growth, and management of the practice.
- staff development,
- client base,
- assignment strategies,
- aggressive or conservative nature,
- reputation in the business community, and
- reputation for treatment of staff.

These items must be considered for the long-run; they are *MUCH* more important than people when considering a career through partnership.

It is true that many students begin a career in public ac-counting with no intention of becoming a partner. These students may wish to weigh the people factor more heavily than other criteria. A caution is in order to those "two-year-and-out" students: *NEVER* tell an interviewer or a person met during the office visit that you have any career goal in mind except to become a partner in the firm. Why? Simple, staff and interviewers do not want to hear it, and may decide not to extend an offer because of this "short-timer" attitude.

Let's review: the reasons for an office visit are for the firm to sell itself to the student and for the student to sell himself or herself to the firm (obtain an offer), then and only then, for each to evaluate the other.

Since the firm's representatives are "on their own turf" in their office and since they realize that their purpose is to sell the firm, they will do most of the talking. Their presentation will give the positive attributes of their firm, office and staff in addition to reasons why a student should begin employment there.

Students, on the other hand, will listen (mainly), smile, nod their head, use appropriate listening techniques (i.e., body language, eye contact, attentiveness, etc., as described in Chapter 4), and almost always be asked, "Do you have any questions?" A student *MUST* have questions for each person met during the day on the subject being discussed for, in all honesty, these questions and most importantly their quality are the very points upon which the student is being evaluated and judged. Why? Auditors by nature are curious, inquisitive people. It is their business to ask questions; therefore, they expect questions during an office visit. Additionally, questions show that a student is genuinely interested both in a career in public accounting and in the particular firm he is visiting; conversely, the lack of questions signifies a lack of interest in the profession which will generate a lack of interest in the student by the firm.

Ask questions! But ask questions which are intelligent. Show a genuine interest. You should not have to think too hard about appropriate questions. A forty year career in an environment as diverse and exciting as public accounting should generate literally *hundreds* of questions.

Now let's look at a typical office visit to give you an idea of what to expect. What you are about to read is an office visit sequence used by many offices. It is similar in organization to office visits of any office of any firm and has actually been excerpted and modified for use today in the Big-8 firms and also several national, regional and local firms across the United States.

TYPICAL OFFICE VISIT PROGRAM

ABC & COMPANY
INTERNAL COMMUNICATION

ABC & Company
123 Debit Boulevard
Denver, Colorado

Date: October 26, 19XX

To: Office Visit Participants

From:

Subject: Outline for Office Visits

The office visit is the most critical phase of our recruiting program because it is the basis for decision by both the student and the Firm. It is our best opportunity to "sell" ABC & Company and our Denver office.

We have selected you to participate in the recruiting program by participating in student office visits. You have a significant responsibility to the student and to the Firm. For the short time you will be with the student, you represent many individual employees of ABC & Company. Be candid; but most of all, be enthusiastic about yourself and the Firm.

You must present "us" to the student as we actually are—a group of individuals whose respect for one another, whose desire to serve our clients to the best of our ability, and whose reputation within the profession and the business community combine to provide an atmosphere of challenge, recognition and opportunity for advancement.

The students who interest us generally receive offers from several of the major firms. We believe that the characteristics and policies of our Firm compare favorably with those of any of the others. Our presentations to the student should emphasize the differences which we believe are significant in distinguishing our Firm from the other major accounting firms.

The attached Exhibits detail our approach to the office visit. Become familiar with the entire sequence; prepare your presentation in detail.

Exhibit 1 — General arrangements for an office visit
Exhibit 2 — Outline of presentation
Exhibit 3 — Evaluation form
Exhibit 4 — Expense reimbursement form
Exhibit 5 — Facts & Figures

Exhibit 1

ARRANGEMENTS

The letter inviting a student to visit our office will ask the student to call the Director of Recruiting (collect) to set a mutually convenient date for the office visit. This letter is typed by Personnel and signed by the campus recruiter. When a student calls, the following points are covered:

. . . . Time and expected length of visit—usually 10:00 A.M. to 3:00 P.M. or 11: A.M. to 4:00 P.M.

. . . . Hotel and transportation reservations—Offer to make reservations at the hotel if an overnight stay is involved. It is best to allow the student to make his own travel arrangements after we forward an appropriate advance with our confirming letter.

. . . . Out-of-town students can be met at the hotel or in our office at the time of the interview. Experience dictates that meeting for breakfast at the hotel is appropriate and convenient. Dinner with staff is most desirable if time permits.

Personnel is responsible for certain arrangements prior to the student visit:

. . . . Benefits Summary, several annual reports, staff training binder and a recruiting brochure should be available.

. . . . Student Kit (handout) should be completed as outlined in the "Greeting and Orientation" section of the Outline.

. . . . Send letter confirming time and date to each student two weeks prior to appointment.

Exhibit 2

CONDUCTING THE VISIT

The Office Visit Outline should only be used as a guide in speaking with the student. Never follow it verbatim. "Necessary materials" may be obtained from Personnel if not readily available. Inject personal experiences as relevant, but remember always that the student should do half the talking. Don't be afraid to SMILE . . . PLEASE!

Once you have completed your topic within the approximate time constraints of the outline, introduce the student to the next team member on the schedule, complete an Interviewer Impressions form and take it to Personnel immediately.

Lunches should be casual and as stress free for the student. Always bear in mind, however, that you are always "selling" ABC & Company. Staff responsible for lunches should make luncheon reservations through the Director's secretary. After lunch, account for your expenses and complete the Interviewer's Impression Form, which is to be given to Personnel.

FOLLOW-UP

Once the visit is completed, Personnel will form a consensus opinion from the evaluations prepared by each team member. Based on this opinion, a decision will be made as to whether an offer should be made. All offers will be made verbally and confirmed in a letter sent by Personnel.

OFFICE VISIT OUTLINE

The following pages contain an outline of the important topics that will be covered in the office visit of each student. As a team member, you should become familiar with the entire outline so as to know the sequence and topics covered by each team member. Become completely familiar with your assigned topic so that you can present it with enthusiasm.

Exhibit 2

GREETING & ORIENTATION
APPROXIMATELY ½ HOUR
(Personnel Director or Campus Recruiter)

GREETING

- General conversation to put the student at ease; offer coffee, tea, etc.

REIMBURSEMENT EXPENSES

- Complete "Applicant Expenses Statement" form
- Account for any funds advanced to student.

OUTLINE AGENDA FOR THE DAY

- Preview agenda, discussion topics and background of firm personnel to be met.
- Be certain that there is sufficient time to meet plane or other travel schedules.

INQUIRE IF THERE ARE ANY PRESSING QUESTIONS

NECESSARY MATERIALS

STUDENT KIT (HANDOUT):

- Applicant Expense Statement
- Recruiting Brochure
- Benefit Summary
- Performance Reports
- Agenda for day's visit, including resumes where applicable
- Latest technical publications

Exhibit 2

EMPLOYEE BENEFITS AND RELATED MATTERS
(15 minutes—if applicable)
(Personnel Director)

BENEFITS SUMMARY

- Let the student see the Summary while significant matters of interest are discussed.

VACATIONS AND HOLIDAYS

- Using Summary, describe the Firm's vacation policy.
- Point out holidays observed.

INSURANCE

- Blue Cross/Blue Shield
  Emphasize that Firm pays most of the premium for employee and dependents. Cost for family is $xx.xx per month, $x.xx for individuals.

- Other insurance
  Using Handbook, describe life insurance coverage and premium for different salary ranges.

- Describe short-term and long-term disability insurance.

- Travel Insurance—Note coverage and that there is no cost to employee.

MEMBERSHIP AND DUES

- AICPA and state society dues are paid by the Firm.
- Certain related dinners and social activities are paid.

SOCIAL ACTIVITIES

- Believe in hard work and hard play—dinner dance, Christmas party, softball (men and women), golf, tennis and bridge teams, other Firm sponsored employee and family-oriented activities.

RETIREMENT PLAN

- Mention that we have such a plan.

TRAVEL

- Average number of nights out of town—probably about ten percent.
- Little travel outside of state.
- Auto usage reimbursed at $.XX per mile.
- Our staff is expected to live and travel as professionals while on Firm business.
- Travel advances are provided, if necessary.

MATCHING GIFTS PROGRAM

- Firm will match gifts to colleges of your choice.

OVERTIME

- Discuss extent of overtime; mention our management objective to control overtime and spread it evenly through the staff.
- Describe method of compensation for overtime. Overtime for staff below managers is "banked" and paid at year end (straight time rates). Overtime worked in excess of 120 hour bank is paid on a monthly basis. Firm may request you take overtime off in lieu of payment during slow periods. In addition, you may request time off in lieu of payment at a mutually convenient time.

OFFICE HOURS

- 8:30 A.M. to 5:00 P.M.
- Normal workweek is 37.5 hours and overtime is paid after 40 hours.

SALARY

- Our salary offers are competitive with other national firms.

NECESSARY MATERIALS

- Benefits Summary
- Personnel Manual

Exhibit 2

ORGANIZATION & CLIENTELE
30-45 Minutes
(Manager or Supervisor)

HISTORY

- Established in Denver in 1920
- Among the largest CPA firms in the country.

ORGANIZATION

- NATIONAL
    - Over 30 offices
    - About 200 partners
    - Nearly 4,000 personnel

- DENVER
    - Size of Denver office
    - Emphasize that we offer a full range of services in Denver and explain role of each:
        - Audit
        - Tax
        - MAS (See Exhibit 5)
        - Small Business Services
        - International and SEC for large clients
    - One of the largest offices in the Firm and in the state.
        - Large enough for vast career and advancement opportunities; yet geared for individual attention.

CLIENTELE

- NATIONAL
    - Extremely diversified base of very small and medium-sized businesses as well as large corporate clients.
    - Hundreds of small and medium-sized clients in various industries. This allows for diversity of work.

CAREER OPPORTUNITIES

- Classifications—Title and general time for promotions
  - Partners—8-12 years after hire
  - Managers—5-7 years after hire
  - Senior—Approximately 2-5 years after hire
  - Senior Assistant—6 months to 1 year
  - Staff Accountant—Upon hire
  - Promotions effective at July 1 of each year.
  - These guidelines for promotion represent neither minimums nor maximums but rather the time it has generally taken ABC & Company staff persons to advance. The Firm imposes no rule as to time-in-grade. Promotions are based on performance.
  - Transfers do occur and may be initiated by the Firm or the individual.
- Transfers from the audit staff into one of the specialty departments (i.e., Tax, MAS) are definite possibilities and generally take place in the second to fourth year of your career.
- Audit Staff Assignments
  - Stress opportunity for broad, diversified experience.
    - Small businesses for perspective; larger businesses for other experience.
    - Opportunity to serve clients with highly sophisticated internal accounting and reporting systems using the most advanced data processing equipment.
    - Opportunity to render constructive services to all clients, particularly small clients; or use advanced auditing & EDP techniques such as:
      - Computer Audit Software Package
      - The Foreign Corrupt Practices Act
      - Software packages

Exhibit 2

OFFICE TOUR
APPROXIMATELY 30 MINUTES
(Staff Accountant)

KEY AREAS TO COVER

- On 18th Floor
  - MAS
  - Accounting
  - IBM 5110 Microcomputer
  - Training Room
  - Tax Department
  - Library
- On 19th Floor
  - Word Processing—IBM System, 6 units (new telecommunications system)
  - Lounge
  - Personnel—explain computer scheduling
  - Managing Partner's office location
  - Conference Room
- During tour of office, introduce student to a few members of management and staff personnel whom the student is not scheduled to meet (try for at least 3 introductions).
- Show and be proud of extensive art work throughout office.

Exhibit 2

ASSIGNMENTS & EVALUATIONS
(AT LUNCH)
(Staff Accountant and Senior Assistant)

ASSIGNMENTS

- Emphasize diversification policy; mention that:
  - We want to develop individual's broad capabilities through diversified assignments.
  - Individual annual assignments include small as well as large engagements and a variety of audit and accounting work in several different industries.
  - Assignment teams are formed for each engagement only, but assignments are made centrally so that staff will work with as many different seniors and managers as possible; in as many industries and as many different size engagements as possible (very important to stress at this point).
  - No one is assigned exclusively to one engagement.

EVALUATION

- Comment briefly on the importance of the evaluation process; stress importance to the individual.
- Describe briefly our procedure
  - Evaluation at conclusion of each engagement. Show copies of performance reports and description of evaluation procedure.
  - Annual Personnel Interview. Describe briefly how it works.
- Review in May for July 1 promotions.

NOTES:

- Lunch should be friendly and informal (this is more important than covering any topic.)
- Drinks—we as hosts must set tone for drinks. One drink is appropriate and the student should be so informed.

Exhibit 2

CONTINUING PROFESSIONAL EDUCATION
AND QUALITY CONTROL
(30-45 Minutes)
(SENIOR)

State briefly firm's commitment and Denver's commitment to staff training.

Describe briefly national training programs for new staff, emphasize purpose and content. Show pamphlets and training manual.

- National meeting(s)
- Local meetings

Describe Denver office training program

- Show schedule. Point out where he will fit in now; where he will fit in as career progress is made.
- Mention CPA coaching course and that our results have been outstanding. (Over 50 percent of parts taken are passed.)
- Be sure to mention special training sessions like Senior's Technical Sessions.
- Mention Tax courses, APB's, FASB's, Banking Seminar, Insurance and nonprofit seminars, and self-study courses.

Mention educational materials he will receive (these are displayed in Personnel area and Library).

- Accounting & Auditing Policy
- Tax Manuals, Newsletter, Handbooks

Mention Firm's leadership in technical developments such as:

- Retail Audits
- Systems
- Computer Auditing

If there is interest, mention

- Annual meetings of Partners and Managers
- Management Seminar for Partners
- Seminars for training directors
- Meeting of Tax, MAS, other specialists
- Tax Symposium and seminar for Tax Department

Discuss importance of on-the-job training and how this is where the learning curve will be the steepest.

Discuss CPA requirements and review course

Quality control review program

- Local
- National

Discuss how everyone is involved through workpaper preparation; workpaper review.

Exhibit 2

OPPORTUNITY AND ADVANCEMENT
(15 Minutes)
(Partner)

NOTE: The content of this subject will vary with the caliber and interest of the student.

Summarize briefly what we have to offer

- Clientele—Assert that our practice is unequalled in its diversity of industries, size, SEC practice, etc.

- Training—Reiterate management's commitment to an outstanding training program.

- Growth—Growth is opportunity, not anonymity.

- Emphasize potential for rapid advancement. If student is clearly outstanding, be certain that he understands that he will receive the opportunities to help him move as fast as possible.

- Technical excellence of the Firm.

Try to convey the spirit of our Firm—friendly yet professional.

If the student is interested in specific issues affecting the profession such as encroachment or advertising, you may want to discuss the firm's positions. In addition, describe how firm policy on these issues is set.

- Briefly reiterate rate of advancement:
  - Manager—5-7 years
  - Partner—8-12 years

Other information

- Turnover—We experience approximately the same turnover as other firms which runs about 20 percent annually.

Exhibit 2

CLOSE
(15 Minutes)
(Personnel Director)

ATTITUDE

- Evaluate student's attitude toward Firm and its personnel
- Assess expected offer

Describe further contact procedure

Reimburse expenses

OFFER TO STUDENT

- Use of library
- Mailing list inclusion
- Second interview

OFFER OF EMPLOYMENT MAY BE MADE

Exhibit 3

INTERVIEW IMPRESSIONS
(Hand Carry to Personnel Immediately After Interview)

Date .... Candidate ....

Interviewer .... Topic ....

Assessment of Candidate:	Unacceptable	Acceptable	Good	Very Good	Outstanding
Quality of questions asked	___	___	___	___	___
Enthusiasm displayed	___	___	___	___	___
Assertiveness/Self confidence	___	___	___	___	___
Maturity/Common sense	___	___	___	___	___
Drive/Desire to achieve	___	___	___	___	___
Leadership potential	___	___	___	___	___
Motivation for *career* in P.A.	___	___	___	___	___

Rank the candidate in comparison to your perception of his/her relative POTENTIAL among all candidates in the Market:

Upper 10% ___ Upper Third ___ Middle Third ___ Lower Third ___

Would you extend an offer?   Yes ___ No ___

Do you feel that you developed enough rapport
to be effective in follow-up activities?   Yes ___ No ___

Do you want to be active in follow-up?   Yes ___ No ___

Significant comments: ....

Exhibit 4

__ CHECK __ CASH REQUISITION
and
APPLICANT EXPENSE STATEMENT

Amount ....   Date ....

Payable to: ....

....

For: Employment Visit to ABC & Company Denver Office

....

Requested by: ....   Charge to: 0004327

Approval: ....

Disposition: ....

DETAIL	Total	
Plane, Bus, Airport Limousine, Taxi, Auto Hire		
Number of Miles by Auto (x .xxx)		
Hotel Room Charge		
Meals: __Breakfast, __Lunch, __Dinner		
Baggage, Tips, and Parking Fees		
Other		
Less Advance from ABC		
Total		

Exhibit 5

SMALL BUSINESS DEPARTMENT (SBD)

The Small Business Department has been established to provide a broad range of auditing and accounting, tax, consulting, financial and business advisory services to smaller and medium-sized businesses on a personalized basis and at a level of quality consistent with the Firm. We have entered this market in the Denver office with approximately 15 professionals (partners and staff at all levels) working full- and/or part-time.

The reasons for our continued heavy involvement in the SBD area are:

- To develop potential for larger-sized clients
- To fulfill our full-service commitment
- To obtain increased revenues
- To enhance staff development

MANAGEMENT ADVISORY SERVICES (MAS)

- The MAS Group is made up of nearly 75 consultants spread nationally into 5 offices.
- Centralized personnel and career planning provides:
  - Broadest possible type of consulting experience encompassing many industries, with an average engagement duration of four weeks.
  - Most consultants have ten years of experience.
  - Consultants deal at the highest levels (President, COB, etc.) Very little "turn-key" consulting.

Exhibit 5

TAX DEPARTMENT

The Tax Department's primary focus is to do tax planning and problem solving. In addition, the department reviews accruals and all returns. Returns are prepared by audit staff to broaden knowledge.

CLOSING

Because of the dynamic nature of college recruiting, this office visit sequence will change from time to time. We solicit your comments for change and thank you for your cooperation.

EXPENSE REIMBURSEMENTS

The current practice of national firms and many regional and local firms is to reimburse you for actual out-of-pocket expenses incurred in connection with your office visit. Reimbursements are made for plane, train or bus fares, auto mileage (at the same rate per mile which the office reimburses its staff), parking, meals while traveling, hotel (if necessary for your visit) and any other reasonable expense necessary for your trip. These are legitimate business expenses for the firm and you should not be bashful or ashamed to expect reimbursement. The key word with respect to expenses is "reasonable." In other words, do not eat hamburgers every meal and do not order $40.00 steaks.

Expenses will either be reimbursed by cash or check at the conclusion of your office visit or will be mailed to you in one to three weeks. If it is necessary to submit an expense report to the firm after your visit, do so immediately. The sooner you submit your report, the sooner you will be reimbursed. Incidentally, you should have receipts for all expenditures, but you *MUST* have them for hotel accommodations, air fares and all expenses exceeding $25.00.

OFFICE VISIT PERCEPTIONS

During your visit, you will be "bombarded" with information about the firm. The astute student will go beyond the obvious when assessing specific firms. Some areas to watch for: Are the partners' offices segregated from the rest of the managers and staff or spread throughout the office? Are most office doors open or closed? During the tour, were you introduced to personnel not on your schedule? Did people nod or say "hello" in the hallway? Did individuals address each other (and partners) on a first name basis? Did you get the impression that most firm members knew one another? At the in-charge accountant and staff levels, were there a lot of staff in the office at their desks (as opposed to assigned at client locations?) Remember that 85% of all auditing is done at the client's business by staff below the Partner/Manager level—too many people available in the office may suggest not enough work to go around. To what extent were you impressed by the honesty of people describing the "pros" and "cons" of the profession and firm?

While it will be impossible to know all there is to know about a firm in a 5 or 6 hour visit, your perceptivity about the environment can reveal a great deal to aid your decision process once you receive an offer.

SUMMARY

Both the firm and the student are selling each other during the office visit. Each is also evaluating the other. The student must meet the same criteria as the interviewer regarding appearance, dress, enthusiasm and interest. Also, the student must be prepared to ask intelligent questions and gather enough information upon which to base an employment decision. *YOUR GOAL IS TO RECEIVE AN OFFER.*

6 OFFER AND DECISION

Let's assume you are completing an office visit and are ushered into the personnel director's office. At this point, the director has preliminary and perhaps final evaluations on you; and you have some idea as to what you think of the firm, office and staff. What happens next?

CLOSING THE OFFICE VISIT

The personnel director will "close" the office visit. In a sense, he is trying to get you to "sign on the dotted line." Usually the close will consist of a summary of the strengths of the firm and office, a statement of how well you would fit in and why you should work there. You will be reimbursed for your out-of-pocket travel expenses and offered the opportunity to call the office should further questions develop. You may even be offered the use of the office's library, be put on a mailing list for firm literature or be offered copies of newspapers (if you are from another city).

99

Whatever happens, the intent is to make you feel like you already joined the staff—you have found a home.

During the closing you will be asked what you think of the firm, office and staff. Be positive in your response ("I like it," "I want to work here," etc.) for you still do not have an offer.

Questions pertaining to your other interview successes will be asked. At this point, do not be modest. Honestly state the success you have had. Imply that you are being sought after by several firms (i.e., "I've visited four firms and have three offers so far and have my last two office visits next week" or "This is my first office visit. So far I have a total of six invitations.")

Some interviewers will ask you for the exact amount of your previous salary offers. You are under no obligation to divulge that information and probably should not. By asking your exact salary offers, the interviewer is attempting to find out what the competition is offering as well as the value placed on you by other firms. Usually, the interviewer's main intent is to make sure their offer is competitive. In effect, they desire to take salary out of your decision equation. That is to say, if all of your offers are for the same amount, then your decision on which firm to join must be made on the basis of factors other than money. Firms do not want you to think that the only way they can hire good people is to pay you more than everyone else. Recognizing this may result in your deciding to share other offer amounts.

On the other hand, there are some good reasons *not* to divulge other offer amounts.

If another firm values you below the market, you become "tainted" (Why are you below the market?). If your offers place you above the average market value, you may be out of range and will not be expected to accept a lower offer—so why should this firm make one? You may want this firm at a lower offer! Additionally, the interviewer should know current starting salaries through ethical sources, or should be willing to set his own standards regardless of the competition.

However, if you are asked and have decided not to divulge your offers, simply and boldly say, "I have a great interest in your firm and am sure that if I am fortunate enough to receive an offer, it will be fair and competitive in the marketplace." If the interviewer persists, say "I do not want a discussion of starting salary to hamper my chances at receiving an offer from your firm, but I will not discuss my other offers which I think are both competitive and quite satisfactory."

One last word on offer amounts. There will be hundreds of factors to consider in your decision of which offer to accept. Starting salary is only one factor and should be kept in perspective. A $500 or $1,000 differential is inconsequential compared to the grief you experience after choosing a firm which does not meet your career needs, despite the initial pleasure of making more money than your fellow graduates. If the firm that is most appealing to you makes a low salary offer which is standing in the way of your acceptance, then by all means discuss your other offers with the appropriate individual. Chances are very good that they did not realize their offer was not competitive and accordingly, will increase the offer without feeling unduly pressured.

OFFERS

You will learn the results of your office visits in one of three ways. You will receive:

- Offers in the office.
- Offers by letter.
- Letters of rejection.

OFFER IN THE OFFICE

At the conclusion of your office visit, you may be extended a verbal offer of employment which will be confirmed to you in writing. You are not expected to accept or reject a verbal offer when it is made; but you will be expected to make a decision by a specific date—normally within four to six weeks of the office visit. This should give you adequate time both to complete your office visits with other firms and to make your final decision. If for some reason this is not enough time to complete your other interviews, most firms will extend the date if asked. If you receive a lot of pressure from a firm to accept an offer immediately or it will be rescinded, inform your placement office. Most employees agree to operate under College Placement Council standards which require students to be given a reasonable amount of time to complete interviews and make a decision. Employers exerting unreasonable pressure are generally trying to "pluck you out of the marketplace" before you have a chance to see the quality firms and opportunities available to you. This strategy is unprofessional and should lead you to question whether this is the type of firm for which you would want to work.

OFFER BY LETTER

The policy in some firms dictates that offers not be made in the office during the close. Or, because the summary of your evaluations may not be complete in time for the closing, you may not receive a verbal offer in the office. In no way does this mean that you will not be extended an offer or that the firm's desire to have you join their staff has diminished. If you do not receive an offer in the office, you will probably be told to expect to hear favorably within a few days (usually less than 10 days). You will then receive your offer in the mail.

REJECTION LETTER

As has been stated, about 30% of all office visits result in rejection letters. Reasons are too numerous to mention; but it's possible that:

- you interviewed poorly,
- did not "fit" the office,
- the campus interviewer invited the wrong person, or
- the firm has already completed its hiring.

Do not be discouraged by one or two rejection letters—almost everyone receives that number. On the other hand, if you have received eight to ten rejection letters, immediately seek faculty and placement office help.

FOLLOW-UP ACTIVITIES

Once you have received an offer from a firm, you will probably be subjected to follow-up activities. If you like, an offer is like a marriage proposal, the follow-up is like the courtship and the acceptance is like marriage. The courtship, in this case the follow-up activities, can take various forms: lunches, dinners, sporting events, phone calls (usually early in the morning or late at night because students are difficult to reach during the day), etc. It all sounds great! But let four or six firms begin to "wine-and-dine" you and it will get boring very quickly, cut into your normal social life and could hurt your studies. Do not hesitate to request that firms stop this "badgering" (they will not withdraw their offer and may really prefer not to engage in follow-up anyway).

Some firms as a matter of policy will not do follow-up as a service to the student. Extending you an offer states intention and conviction: "You are a mature adult about to enter the business world and do not need someone to hold your hand. You will not be badgered by us."

Whatever a firm does with regard to follow-up, do not be swayed from your long-range objectives by a free meal or a phone call. The offer itself says it all! Also, do not be disillusioned by all of the attention and money spent on you. Regardless which firm you ultimately join, you begin at the bottom rung of the ladder. You will be assigned both challenging and routine responsibilities, but recognize the courtship is over and each day of your "married life" will not include theater tickets and filet mignon at the Ritz. Any employer who tells you otherwise is being less than honest.

DECISION

If all has gone well with your interviews, at this point you have several offers. Now comes the enjoyable but difficult task of deciding which firm to join.

IT IS NOW TIME TO BE YOURSELF—to compare your real needs, wants, desires, habits and personality with what each firm has to offer you. This is an important decision.

To assist you quantify a truly subjective decision, a Decision Matrix is presented on the next page. Use it as a guideline in making your decision. You will note that the "People Bonus," added at the end, is limited. This is intentional because it is felt that too many students are swayed in their decision by the "people" met during the office visit. This is important only in terms of "types of people" employed at a firm versus specific individuals whom you met. Frankly, everyone you meet during an office visit will probably have terminated employment before you become a partner. Therefore, your long-range interests are best served by looking well beyond the people. Look at firm philosophy, policies, procedures, audit and managerial approach, growth, etc., and relate them to your own goals, needs, wants and desires. Then, and only then, look at the people. Of course, be happy with them and be able to get along with them; but do not make the mistake of basing your entire career decision on five or six people who probably won't be around as long as you will.

Now try the Matrix! Use the notes you compiled on the Interview Log after each campus interview and office visit. Rate each factor.

Good Luck!

Once you have made your decision, call (collect) the firm you have chosen and accept the offer. Confirm your acceptance in writing. Then call or write the other firms to reject their offers. Most firms that you reject will try very hard to find out which firm's offer you accepted. To save yourself time, you may wish to advise them of which firm you are joining in your letter (telephone call). Reject their offers professionally and with gratitude. You never know what your needs will be tomorrow.

DECISION MATRIX

Rating value:

- -1 — Turned me off
- 0 — Does not matter, or
      same for all, or
      don't care
- +1 — O.K.
- +2 — Great! Just what I wanted (or needed)!

Rate each of the following with the above points for each firm from which you received an offer. Total each firm's points and use the results as input to your final decision which in the final analysis you must make yourself.

FIRMS

Offer:

Size:
- Worldwide
- Domestic Practice
- Local Office
    - Audit
    - Tax
    - Consulting
    - Computer Science
    - Small Business
    - Administration

Revenue:
- Worldwide
- Domestic Practice
- Local Office

Number of Offices:
- Worldwide
- Domestic Practice
- My State

106

	FIRMS										
Growth (last 5, 10 years):										
Worldwide										
Domestic Practice										
Local Office:										
Potential Market										
Internal Growth										
Merger Activity										
Aggressiveness										
Clients:										
Total Number										
Number SEC										
Number Small Business										
Variety or Mix										
Number of 1040's										
Number of 1120's										
Assignments:										
Average Length										
Longest										
Shortest										
How Made										
How Far in Advance										
Specialization										
Rotation Policy										
No. 1st-year Assignments										
Who Prepares Tax Returns										
Evaluations:										
Procedures										
Frequency										
Feedback System										
Management (no., age, ratio)										
Partners										
Managers										

	FIRMS									
Supervisors										
Seniors										
Staff										
Transferability:										
To Another Office										
Tax										
Consulting										
Computer Group										
International Practice										
Continuing Professional Education Courses:										
National										
Local										
Orientation										
Specialization										
Computer										
Workpaper Preparation										
CPA Review										
AICPA										
State Society										
Number of Hours/Year										
Study in Unassigned Time										
Who Coordinates										
Compensation:										
Review Frequency										
Profit Sharing										
Bonus										
Overtime Payment										
Formula										
Rate/Hour										
Average Hrs—1st Year										
Average Hrs—Seniors										
Average Hrs—Mgmt.										

FIRMS

Fringe Benefits:
    Vacation
    Holidays
    Pension
    Health Insurance
    HMO (Health Maintenance
        Organization)
    Life Insurance
    Accidental Death
    Short-Term Disability
    Long-Term Disability
    Professional Dues
    Meetings Expenses
    Tuition Aid
    CPA Coaching Course
    Social Activities
    Office Hours
    Parking Fees at Office

Travel:
    Number of Nights/Year
    To Where
    Expense Advances
    Charge Card Provided
    Car Rental Policy
    Plane Tickets
    Hotel Bills
    Meal Allowances
    Mileage Allowance
    Reimbursement Formula
    Parking Fees at Clients'

Turnover:
    Rate
    From What Level

109

	FIRMS								
Out-Placement Services									
Rehire Policy									
Last Layoff									
No. Counsel-Outs/Year									
Termination Procedures									
Miscellaneous:									
Personality of Office									
Liberal									
Conservative									
Friendly									
Enthusiastic									
Relaxed									
Stuffy									
Individualism Encouraged									
Nepotism Policy									
Number of Females									
Number of Minorities									
Office Appearance:									
Neat									
Professional									
Bright									
Cheerful									
Subtotal									
People Bonus ("They're my kind of people) 2 points maximum									
TOTAL									

REMEMBER, YOU ARE MAKING AN INVESTMENT IN TIME
(ABOUT 100,000 WAKING HOURS), MONEY ($8,000,000)
AND IN YOUR OWN FUTURE.

MAKE THE RIGHT DECISION!

7 PROFESSION

Public accounting in the United Sates began at about the turn of the century and has grown quietly (due to its nonadvertising ethic) to the point where several worldwide firms enjoy revenues of over one billion dollars per year.

BIG 8

Years ago a national magazine coined the phrase "Big 8" to describe the largest of these firms. They are partnerships with international headquarters in the U. S. and Europe. Some employ in excess of 30,000 people. All practice or have correspondent or affiliate offices in most countries of the free world. In alphabetical order they are: Arthur Andersen & Co.; Arthur Young & Co.; Coopers & Lybrand; Deloitte Haskins & Sells; Ernst & Whinney; Peat, Marwick, Main & Co.; Price Waterhouse & Co.; and Touche Ross & Co.

Each of these firms offer outstanding career opportunities in audit, tax or consulting for the student with the proper credentials. Also, each firm has its own personality, level of allowable specialization and reward system. Each also attempts to hire the best students on campus.

BIG 15

After the Big 8, about seven firms provide formidable competition in scope and breadth of practice but are smaller in size though also international. Career opportunities abound in these often overlooked firms. A hard-charging student not willing to put up with the supposed rigidity of the Big 8 could consider one of these firms.

REGIONAL AND LOCAL

Everything from sole practitioners up to large firms with many offices and hundreds of staff falls in this category. Most firms begin as sole practitioners; many grow. The larger of these firms offer a full range of services—audit, tax and consulting; but as size shrinks, so does the variety of services. All offer accounting, audit and tax services; consulting is usually the last client service to be offered.

ASSOCIATIONS

It has not been uncommon for successful local or regional CPA firms to join together in the form of professional associations. Historically, distance from divisions of certain clients, prestige, scope of services, breadth of technical resources and other sound business reasons lead smaller firms to work together for their mutual benefit. Competition for clients was usually avoided because of the distance between firms. Several associations of smaller firms exist today whose combined manpower rival the size of national firms.

Recent developments have led to the formation of a great number of new associations or groups. The high cost of mandatory Continuing Professional Education, Technical Standards, Peer Review, etc. has become a financial burden on each individual firm. Joined together in an association, however, smaller firms can provide themselves with a broader technical base in terms of client service as well as providing quality in-house training for its staff, at a lower cost to each firm. The number of associations is growing rapidly.

An individual firm belonging to an association should not be overlooked because the firm is small. The combined strength of the association's practice may provide you with the challenge your career requires.

Most students completely overlook these firms—so sad! Part of the reason is because most of the small firms do not recruit on campus. They are unable or unwilling to devote the time and resources to recruiting; and more often than not, they are unable to provide new employees with in-house continuing professional education. However, a candidate willing to devote the time to formal training outside the firm (i.e., state society, local college, etc.) will usually assume responsibility faster, deal with higher levels of client management sooner and gain more audit, accounting, consulting and taxation expertise quicker in a small firm's relaxed atmosphere.

It should be quickly pointed out that most of the larger local and most regional firms offer all the training, services and advantages of the big firms, usually without the formal atmosphere.

A caution: assure yourself that the number of partners or the number in the ''pipeline'' ahead of you is not so great that the net profit pie is cut too many times—leaving only a small slice for each partner. This same caution, of course, should be considered for any potential employer.

SERVICES

AUDIT AND ACCOUNTING

Client services include everything from simple bookkeeping through issuing opinions on the financial statements of the country's largest corporations. To compete with smaller firms in service and fee, some of the larger firms have formed small business departments to service small and emerging businesses. Others handle both small and large clients with their general audit staff.

Many larger firms have developed other specialty areas under the "umbrella" of, and as a natural outgrowth of accounting and auditing services. These may include Merger and Acquisition services, litigation support, strategic financial planning valuation services, and other specialties under the broad category of financial analysis. Each of these areas require individuals to have a sound background in auditing and solid understanding of business operations. Generally, a person involved in providing these services would also maintain a reduced audit client base. The point is, today's business environment is complex and demands that each CPA excel as a business advisor/consultant in addition to providing a quality audit. For these reasons, public accounting ranks high as a profession with limitless opportunities for bright, motivated college graduates.

Industry specialties have also developed (i.e., insurance, banking, retail, etc.). Special departments such as those for micro-computer or computer auditing have been formed. Some firms will "career path" you into one of these special groups immediately while other firms believe in diversity of experience—at least for a year or two.

About 85 percent of the entrants into public accounting will join an audit staff. Throughout your career, actual training, working, learning experiences and evaluations may lead you toward an eventual specialization.

TAX

The tax department in a CPA firm is generally responsible for tax compliance (return preparation), planning and research. Depending on the management philosophy, returns may be prepared by audit staff and checked by tax staff or prepared and checked by tax staff. If gaining experience in tax preparation is important to you—ask.

Certain firms believe in hiring predominantly law school graduates into their tax practice due to the amount of tax legal research they do for their clients. These firms will generally transfer an auditor into the tax practice after about two years experience which includes tax return preparation and "light" tax research. Assuming successful performance in these areas, the individual would do the same type of work after the transfer as that done by the law school graduates.

Very few firms hire accounting majors directly into their tax department, but the few that do usually have the new person preparing returns. (Incidentally, the largest single employer of attorneys in the United States outside the Federal Government is a CPA firm.)

It is important to assess each tax practice carefully because they are not all the same. The amount of tax compliance work versus tax research and planning can vary significantly from firm to firm. You must decide what aspects of taxation client service appeal to you and ask questions accordingly.

CONSULTING

Consulting practices in CPA firms have grown through aggressive marketing of certain skills or areas of expertise. Most CPA-firm consultants have become experts in a particular field before becoming consultants. Thus, the number of entry-level consulting positions open to college students is very limited. The few positions going to students go to the top MBAs from nationally recognized graduate schools. There are, of course, exceptions but it must be realized that it is very difficult for those fresh out of college to appear more attractive to a prospective employer than those who have acquired expertise in a certain area. The title "Consultant" can be quite glamorous as well as somewhat misleading. It is important to make sure you have a clear picture of the job responsibilities (i.e., computer programming vs. systems design) including how long it will be before you get any real client contact. This is another example of how important your advance research can be.

Several firms do have special programs to hire recent graduates as consultants, but train them as auditors for a year or two. A small number of auditors with long-range consulting goals may transfer between the two departments each year. Perhaps two to three percent of a group of new employees go directly into consulting, and most of these are with one particular Big-8 firm.

8 INTERNSHIPS

A public accounting internship is a valuable experience for an accounting student. A school term spent in the office of a public accounting firm will provide an accounting major with valuable insights into a potential career as well as the profession.

INTERN'S REASONS

From an intern's point of view, many benefits accrue:

Pay—about $1,500 per month for interns entering their senior year and about $1,900 per month for MBAs. In most cases, overtime is paid.

Experience—Hands-on experience of audit/tax techniques which is beneficial throughout a career as well as during the last year of coursework.

Formal Training—Interns usually attend the same formal training programs as new full-time staff. Between ten and twenty percent of an intern's experience will be in a classroom receiving continuing professional education.

Career Orientation—Exposure to actual work, fellow staff and a professional atmosphere will help a student develop career goals, interview savvy and probably a job offer.

Job—About 90 percent of all interns receive an offer of employment from their intern employer. Between 60 and 85 percent of all interns accept that offer after interviewing (and receiving offers from) other firms.

FIRM'S REASONS

CPA firms are active in internship programs, not **because** they want to be, but because they have to be for **competitive** recruiting reasons. Better students usually seek internships. If the firm wants to be successful in its recruiting efforts next year, it must be active in the intern program this year. Internships, therefore, are viewed by most firms solely as a *RECRUITING TOOL.*

Using internships as a recruiting device is the only way for most firms to economically justify their participation. Business is generally slow in the summer since most clients have a 12/31 year-end. Summer clients are usually made up of non-profit entities (school districts, cities, charitable organizations, etc.) with a 6/30 year-end. Most firms do not make much profit from these clients, however, they do cover firm overhead expenses and provide auditing experience. New permanent staff usually begin their employment in the summer slow season, and often there is not enough work to keep them busy—let alone challenged. Now, add interns to an already underutilized staff—no one is busy or challenged. Why have interns?

Consider this: if you were an audit manager seeking to staff your engagement with the best, most efficient and most productive staff possible, which would you choose: an intern with three or four accounting courses or a degreed accountant with experience on three or four audits? Naturally, you would choose the experienced accountant.

So would an audit manager! The assignments department must go out of its way to "sell" an intern onto an engagement team—a hassle. Why have interns?

As just stated, it is sometimes difficult to assign an intern to any engagement. But an intern must return to school having had meaningful work experience on several audits; so assignments are made carefully—an intern is "added" to the engagement team. This extra "body" probably was not in the budget, not planned for in work assignments, will require individual training and probably will not contribute to the efficiency or profitability of the engagement. The intern gains knowledge and experience but the firm gains little. Why have interns?

What happens when an intern is not assigned to an engagement? Usually, he proofreads, xeroxes, performs self-study, reads magazines or in general does not receive a professional work experience. Few public accounting firms avoid this difficulty completely. What do you think an intern would tell his campus friends (usually the entire senior class of accounting majors) after this kind of nonexperience? Public accounting firms would prefer not to be involved in internships because of the potential downside risks. Why have interns?

Why have interns? Because *RECRUITING COMPETITION* forces most firms to participate (sometimes reluctantly) in the internship program!

A few firms do have a heavy summer practice and take pride in being able to provide meaningful work experience to interns. Your placement office should be able to help you determine where the best opportunities can be found. While all internship opportunities are usually available only in limited numbers, you may stand a better chance at obtaining a winter internship. Winter internships provide a clearer picture of the public accounting profession due to the workload ("busy season") being at its highest point during the year. Since there are fewer December graduates, the firms will likely have a greater need for additional help. If you can organize your class schedule to accommodate taking a semester off, a winter internship is probably your best bet.

Interviewing for internships is handled the same as for full-time employment, however, firms may not always schedule a campus interviewing date. If you have completed at least three accounting courses and desire an internship, you should send your resume and letter of interest to firms about 2-3 months prior to the start of the internship.

The method of obtaining an internship varies from campus to campus; but you will stand a better chance to gain one of the limited number of positions if you are at the very top of your class, are a campus leader, are a minority or have some kind of "pull" (know someone). If you are not one of these "chosen ones," try had, but do not count on an internship.

What happens if you do not receive an internship? Most importantly, you have not hurt your chances for a permanent position. In fact, by not interning you may even strengthen your chances of getting multiple offers upon graduation. Consider these facts:

- Between 60 and 85 percent of all interns accept a permanent position with their intern employer.
- The "normal" acceptance rate which firms rely on is 1 in 8, or 12½ percent of all offers made, assuming an equally competitive market.
- If you reduce the "normal" rate of acceptance by 60 to 85 percent a firm only has about a 2 or 3 percent chance of your accepting an offer if you interned with another firm.
- If the firm spends about $500 per office visit, where do you think they would rather spend their money: on a student with "intern-ties" to another firm or on a student who has never had an internship?

If you obtain an internship and are successful at impressing the firm, you will probably receive an offer from that firm; other firms may be reluctant to extend an offer to you because their odds of hiring you are very low. Multiple offers will accrue to you only if, or because, you are outstanding, or based on your powers of persuasion on whether you really are "open" to consider other opportunities. It is difficult to make a fair comparison between a firm you spent 3 months with and one office visit of 5-6 hours.

Students without internship experience do not have to fight these odds and therefore have a good chance at multiple offers.

9 YOUR FIRST YEAR

Your first year in public accounting will be full of joys and frustrations. You will have personal and professional challenges and will meet most with success; no doubt you will also have a few failures. New experiences will abound! In this chapter, several common concerns about first-year experiences will be discussed.

EXPECTATIONS

"What can I expect to happen to me my first year in public accounting?" This is a frequently asked question during both the campus interview and the office visit. Unfortunately, few, if any, firms can give you a direct, specific answer to your question. The answer you are likely to receive will generally resemble this:

Your first day of employment is set aside for administration. You will complete forms, receive

123

manuals, etc. and become familiar with administrative policies and procedures as well as begin to meet our staff. Within a week, you will begin our two-week Staff School where you will become familiar with our audit procedures and techniques. Upon return from Staff School, you will begin field work on current engagements requiring new staff.

Your assignments will be varied as to size, industry and supervision during your first year to give you a broad picture of our practice and allow you maximum opportunities for breadth of experience.

Also during your first year you will attend many formal continuing professional education courses to increase your knowledge of current developments in the firm and the profession. These sessions will continue throughout your career.

Additionally, you will develop friendships and begin to participate in social, professional and civic activities of your choice.

Your first year in our firm is the time to learn the basics of our business which will serve you and the firm well into the future. You will be expected to demonstrate common sense, drive, desire and interest; we will provide you with the necessary challenges. Incidentally, we would like you to pass the CPA exam as quickly as possible.

You can readily see that this answer will fit any firm and is true for all firms. Another interviewer may answer the question as follows:

Your first few days on the job are basically orientation sessions. You will learn administrative procedures that you will use the rest of your career.

Soon after you begin with the firm, you will be whisked away to Staff School for two weeks. The emphasis during the day is learning the fundamentals of our firm's "Approach to Auditing." At night, however, the emphasis changes. Aside from the homework assignments, the time is purely for pleasure. This is a time for you to get together with staff members from all over the country and just have a good time.

The training you receive at Staff School prepares you for your work on client engagements. It will help you to understand the basic terminology used by your Senior. Do not fret if you are unsure of yourself on your first couple of jobs. Everyone is afraid when they initially start working. But as you get adjusted and oriented, things will be easier for you. After a few months, you will feel like a "pro."

It is hard to anticipate what your schedule will look like your first year. To begin with, you will be exposed to various clients involving different industry segments: (i.e., manufacturing, banking, school districts, municipalities, hospitals, etc.). The three to four weeks spent on engagements in these areas give you a feel for the industry as a whole. Many of the engagements you are assigned to in the first year remain your clients for the next three to four years. Within this span of time, you can become an "expert" in identifying the problem areas confronting your particular accounts. As you work with other accounts within the same industry, you begin to focus on the key problem areas right away. Thus, the first year serves as a basis for the next few years. You can anticipate performing preliminary work as well as year-end validation. During your first year you will probably test such accounts as cash, accounts receivable, accounts payable and various expense accounts. As you continue the following year, your responsibilities on the particular engagement increase. The accounts you test will be more difficult. A new staff person begins to do what you did the previous year; so, if there are any questions, you can be of assistance to him.

There will be times when you are not out in the field on assignment. Much of this time will be spent either in self-study or in continuing professional education courses. Since it is required by most states that each member of a CPA firm receive forty hours of CPE a year, most new staff members find that they are able to fulfill the requirement with very little problem. These courses aid in preparation for the CPA exam.

The CPA exam is treated as an engagement twice a year—May and November. As a staff person, it is advantageous to pass the exam as early as possible in your career while you still have free time in your schedule. As the first year rolls on into the second, the exam becomes a menace. It becomes harder to find time to study since you are now so much busier.

The rest of your unscheduled time is spent doing odd jobs around the office. Many times you will foot columns of numbers for managers or xerox copies of workpapers for others. During your first year this spare time may upset you, but later on in your career you will appreciate an occasional slack day.

The first year of your career is a learning process for you and an experimental process for your superiors. It is your responsibility to perform as well as you can within the budget constraints given on the particular engagement. At the same time, you should maintain a positive attitude on the job. Complaining about the job only makes you look bad and doesn't help the situation at all.

Again, this answer could fit most any firm. Basically, you are going to be trained in a classroom, assigned to engagements currently in progress (your starting date will have a bearing on this), be evaluated, paid and expected to perform.

Let's look at training, assignments and evaluations in greater detail.

TRAINING

Public accounting has entitled its training programs "Continuing Professional Education" or, in short, "CPE." The American Institute of Certified Public Accountants (AICPA), most firms and most states require CPE through policy or by license law. Generally, 40 hours of formal classroom instruction is set as an annual minimum.

First-year staff rarely have difficulty completing 40 hours of CPE. The two-week Staff School usually fills more than the minimum requirement, but new staff receive additional hours of classroom instruction in the form of technical updates, tax training, workpaper preparation, computer usage, industry specialization, etc. Add to this any self-study courses which detail audit procedures and you have a tremendous number of CPE hours —normally in excess of 100. Now, add 100-plus hours of preparation for the CPA exam (200 if you sit for the exam twice in the same year) and you amass over a month's time in a classroom.

Without a doubt you will receive a great quantity of CPE hours. That leaves the question of quality. All firms offering CPE have good programs per se, but the quality of instruction in any particular course is only as good as the instructor's knowledge of the subject and ability to teach you. National firms usually prepare their own material, train and evaluate instructors and use the latest audio-visual equipment and instructional techniques. They may even have their own facility for use as an education center. Some smaller firms also have the same capabilities by relying on outside material and instructors.

The quality of all in-house CPE courses with all firms is good in an overall sense. No firm has a tremendous competitive edge over another because of the quality of their CPE programs.

Unfortunately, a very important area of training is rarely discussed in an interview. Some believe that on-the-job training (OJT) is far more valuable than CPE as a learning tool. (These are the ones who support the "give 'em a pencil and an eraser and let 'em make some mistakes" philosophy). As a student, you should explore OJT philosophy with interviewers and recognize that both methods are important for career development.

ASSIGNMENTS

Another frequently asked question in a public accounting interview is, "What type of assignments will I receive?" Answers generally sound the same and include diverse assignments with regard to industry type, size, and number of supervisors, tax and consulting as well as immediate or eventual specialization. Just what you wanted to hear!

Before you get too excited, we'd better look at the assignment process in more detail. Please realize that the *MOST* important goal in the assignment process is to service clients. Therefore, everything else is of secondary importance, including your personal wants, desires and even career needs. Different firms and even different offices within the same firm assign staff to engagements by various methods. There are as many hybrids of the following systems as there are assignment managers, but the three basic methods of assigning staff to the numerous audit engagements of an office are:

POOL
TEAM
INDUSTRY

POOL

In this approach, staff are randomly chosen from the entire pool of available accountants. This is generally considered the best method of assigning staff to engagements provided that proper care is given. Before assigning you, a good assignments manager will consider client needs in terms of required skills and level of competency needed, your developmental needs (i.e., if you have never been involved in an inventory observation, this may be a good opportunity for you), career needs (i.e., the engagement is in the health care industry and you have or have not expressed interest in working in that industry), location (distance from your home to the client), manager requests, staff availability, out-of-town travel, overtime and many others. Although no studies have been conducted, the pool method of assigning staff is probably the most widely used in the profession today. It is popular because it provides the most flexibility for everyone. Clients are serviced properly; staff is able to receive a wide variety of assignments through the normal assignments procedure.

The drawbacks of this system, however, could be devastating to the client and to the staff member's career if not closely monitored and controlled. Clients like to see the same group of auditors in their plant or office several years in a row. When accountants return for several audits (referred to as continuity), they know where files are located, who can answer certain questions, what may be material, etc. In other words, when continuity exists, less training is required because the staff on the engagement can become productive immediately. The firm and the client are desirous of maintaining staff continuity whenever possible.

Sometimes the need for continuity is more important than personal desires.

Continuity is not the only factor that can be a shortcoming of the pool system of assignments. Another is that you may not have a mentor on the staff above you—no one person really looking after your career who can impact directly for your benefit.

TEAM

Your assignments to clients from an office that uses a team approach will work like this: you are assigned to a team of auditors and will work constantly with the same team of individuals as it moves from engagement to engagement. There is a strong belief that this approach is more efficient because the team leader has direct responsibility for keeping you busy. Also, because you are going to work with the same staff continually, they have a vested interest in giving you better on-the-job training. The system works very well as long as you like the staff you work with and like the various engagements you and the team are assigned to.

INDUSTRY

Some offices will assign staff to work on only one industry or to a small group of industries. Usually a team, as just described above, will be confined to engagements involving one industry exclusively. This type of assignment process should only be sought by a student absolutely sure of career goals and aspirations.

Each of these methods of assigning staff exists in public accounting today. You should be aware that different methods do exist. Be prepared to inquire during your interviews if this area is important to your employment decision. It may be in your best interests to request a meeting with the person responsible for staff assignments during the interview process. Make sure you have a solid understanding of the assignments system including methods employed to resolve staffing conflicts and meet individual career development requirements. You should also be aware that, no matter which method your chosen firm uses, assignments will tend to repeat between your second and sixth years because of client continuity requirements. Remember, too, that client requirements will come before your personal desires.

Additionally, you should know that you can have a direct impact on your assignments. You are able to influence the number and type of assignments you receive. You can do this by speaking in a positive, professional manner with the assignments department manager or with an audit manager directly. Showing a genuine interest in your career is very helpful to your career goals.

LENGTH OF ASSIGNMENTS—"STUCK"

"Will I be stuck on a large client?" An interviewer with a large client will deny that you will spend a lot of time on one client whereas an interviewer from a firm or office without a large client may strongly imply that you will be stuck on one client should you work for the large client's auditor. Whom do you believe? What does being "stuck" really mean?

You are stuck on a client when you've spent more time there than you want to spend, but "being stuck" is generally thought about in terms of many months or the better part of a year. However, in some client situations, you may be stuck after two hours or a day. It is a feeling more than an amount of time. Some clients are downright unpleasant to outside auditors and you want out—you are "stuck."

There are large engagements where you will spend four to six weeks or longer and small engagements where you will spend four to six days. You may be stuck on either or neither. The engagement will be the learning experience you make of it—no better, no worse. Probably in excess of 95 percent of all engagements are less than six weeks in duration. Realize that most audits occur outside of the Fortune 500 or Fortune 1000. Even the largest audits are broken up into small segments. Also realize that there are students graduating in every class that desire large SEC engagements rather than smaller clients. You can be confident that the wishes of these students are usually granted. If you want a career in auditing, do not fear or avoid any client, any size—you will learn from each experience. However, if you truly want smaller clients, work for a smaller firm, an office of a large firm with only smaller clients or in the small business department of a large office. The latter is gaining in popularity because it has the advantage of a large firm without many of the perceived disadvantages.

EVALUATIONS

Most CPA firms use some type of form to evaluate the performance of their staff. While there are many types of forms in use, the basic purpose of a performance evaluation is to inform and discuss with a staff member: strengths, weaknesses and constructive suggestions for improvement. The form also serves as an input document for promotion and salary reviews.

Since most firms use a performance evaluation, you should not ask an interviewer "Do you have an evaluation system?" Having done your homework, you can assume that the firm you are interviewing does have a system. Therefore, a better question might be "How effective is your evaluation system?" or "What trouble have you encountered with your evaluation system?" or even "How closely does your written evaluation of a staff member correspond to the grapevine's evaluation?"

Needless to say, written evaluations are necessary and as good as the staff involved make them. The system of evaluation is good in all firms; the people using the system are sometimes imperfect. Examples of system breakdown are:

- When evaluations are given two or more months after an engagement has been completed.
- When mistakes and weaknesses are glossed over rather than discussed.
- When no suggestions as to corrective action are made.
- When there are missing evaluations at promotion review time.
- When written evaluations are not personally discussed ("I'll leave a copy in your mail box.").

- When the grapevine carries a totally different impression of you than your written evaluations (all firms have a grapevine to one extent or another).
- When personality conflicts distort what is an already existing lack of objective criteria.

Regardless of the many pitfalls of evaluation systems, much more good than bad is derived. If each staff member at every level assumes the responsibility for honest, frank and timely evaluation discussions and reporting, the system works. As you are being evaluated, it is also your responsibility to seek (demand, if necessary) performance feedback on a regular basis. This allows you to correct deficiencies before an engagement is completed and avoids the problem of receiving formal performance evaluations which come as a complete surprise.

Several performance evaluation forms in use today have been reproduced with permission for your benefit.

C&L

Confidential
PERFORMANCE REPORT
STAFF ACCOUNTANT

Classification: Staff A ☐ Staff B ☐ Name _____ Evaluated By _____ Date _____

Preliminary ☐ Final ☐ Special ☐ Engagement: _____

From ____ to ____   Total Engagement Hours: _____ Total Hours the Staff Was Assigned: _____
DATES ASSIGNED

Manager_____ Partner _____

Describe Duties Assigned: _____

Was the work assigned: Complex ☐ Difficult ☐ Routine ☐

	OUTSTANDING	ABOVE AVERAGE	SATISFACTORY	NEEDS IMPROVEMENT	UNSATISFACTORY	NOT RATED
TECHNICAL COMPETENCE						
Knowledge and application of accounting and auditing standards						
Knowledge and application of the Firm's Uniform Audit Approach						
Knowledge and application of tax principles and procedures						
Preparation of workpapers						
Identification of management letter comments						
Assistance in preparation of review of reports, footnotes, SEC filings, tax returns						
Recommendations for improvements to the audit program						
Knowledge of the client's business						

Comment _____
_____
_____

	OUTSTANDING	ABOVE AVERAGE	SATISFACTORY	NEEDS IMPROVEMENT	UNSATISFACTORY	NOT RATED
BUSINESS SENSE & ADMINISTRATION OF THE ENGAGEMENT						
Use of own budgeted time to perform assigned tasks						
Promptness in completion of duties assigned						
Keeping ICA advised of progress and difficulties						

Comment _____
_____

	OUTSTANDING	ABOVE AVERAGE	SATISFACTORY	NEEDS IMPROVEMENT	UNSATISFACTORY	NOT RATED
LEADERSHIP						
Attitude, self-motivation, dedication, initiative, accepting responsibility						
Problem-solving, conceptualizing, creativity, imagination						
Judgment, common sense						
Relationship with In-Charge Accountant						
Relationship with staff						
Supervision of others						

Comment _____
_____

Effective 9/76

Reprinted with permission of Coopers & Lybrand (Front)

134

	OUTSTANDING	ABOVE AVERAGE	SATISFACTORY	IMPROVEMENT NEEDS	UNSATISFACTORY	NOT RATED

CONTRIBUTION TO FIRM GROWTH

Knowledge of Firm services						
Relationship with client management						
Identification and communication of client needs and opportunities for special services						

Comment _____

EXECUTIVE PRESENCE

Initial impression created (self-confidence, poise, tact, maturity, appearance)						
Lasting impression created (gains the professional respect and confidence of others)						
General business knowledge						

Comment _____

COMMUNICATION

Speaking (clarity, ease, conciseness)						
Writing (clarity, conciseness, organization)						
Listening (attentiveness, responsiveness, understanding)						

Comment _____

1. Will you ask that this person be reassigned to the engagement next year? ☐ Yes ☐ No — Why not? _____

2. What are this person's significant strengths? _____

3. In what areas does this person require improvement? _____

4. What additional experience or education do you recommend to enhance this person's professional development and performance? _____

5. Is this person ready for more demanding assignments now? ☐ Yes ☐ No

6. How do you rate this person's performance overall?

☐ Outstanding ☐ Above-Average ☐ Satisfactory ☐ Needs Improvement ☐ Unsatisfactory

7. Date performance was discussed _____

Signature of Rater _____ Date _____

Manager Comments _____

Signature of Manager _____ Date _____

Effective 9/78

Reprinted with permission of Coopers & Lybrand (Back)

NAME_____ CLASSIFICATION_____

CLIENT_____ DATES WORKED_____

INDUSTRY_____ AUDITED_____ UNAUDITED_____

DESCRIBE WORK ASSIGNED_____

EVALUATOR_____

HAS THE INDIVIDUAL WORKED ON A: DEMANDING ☐ ROUTINE ☐ ASSIGNMENT?

EXPLAIN:_____

EXCEEDS REQUIREMENTS is characterized by consistently outstanding and exceptional performance. This rating requires an explanatory comment by the Evaluator.

MEETS REQUIREMENTS means that the Evaluatee meets obligations and performs responsibilities in a manner expected of a person at that staff level.

NEEDS IMPROVEMENT indicates that the performance is below that which is normally expected from an individual at that particular person's job level. This rating requires suggestions be indicated to improve performance.

The evaluator must support each caption with specific incidents or remarks.

TECHNICAL KNOWLEDGE:
Did the individual possess adequate technical knowledge to function effectively at the level assigned? Did this knowledge encompass accounting principles, auditing standards, and tax accounting? Has the individual kept current on recent developments and new pronouncements on professional practice matters as they affected this engagement?

	Exceeds Requirements	Meets Requirements	Needs Improvement	Not Applicable
Self-Evaluation:	☐	☐	☐	☐
Evaluator's Rating:	☐	☐	☐	☐

ANALYTICAL ABILITY AND JUDGMENT:
Did the individual recognize problems, develop relevant facts, formulate alternative solutions, and decide on appropriate conclusions? Did the individual distinguish between material and immaterial items? Was the individual practical in adapting theory and experience to the individual circumstances of this client?

	Exceeds Requirements	Meets Requirements	Needs Improvement	Not Applicable
Self-Evaluation:	☐	☐	☐	☐
Evaluator's Rating:	☐	☐	☐	☐

WRITTEN EXPRESSION:
Evaluate the effectiveness of the individual's letters, reports, footnotes, memoranda and other forms of written communication.

	Exceeds Requirements	Meets Requirements	Needs Improvement	Not Applicable
Self-Evaluation:	☐	☐	☐	☐
Evaluator's Rating:	☐	☐	☐	☐

VERBAL EXPRESSION:
In conversation did the individual communicate effectively? Were instructions understood the first time? Did the individual sell ideas, obtain acceptance and action?

	Exceeds Requirements	Meets Requirements	Needs Improvement	Not Applicable
Self-Evaluation:	☐	☐	☐	☐
Evaluator's Rating:	☐	☐	☐	☐

PERFORMANCE:
Can you depend on the individual for sustained, productive work? Were assignments organized and completed accurately in a reasonable amount of time? Did the individual meet time estimates and document work papers properly?

	Exceeds Requirements	Meets Requirements	Needs Improvement	Not Applicable
Self-Evaluation:	☐	☐	☐	☐
Evaluator's Rating:	☐	☐	☐	☐

P-005A (4/79)

Reprinted with permission of Laventhol & Horwath (Front)

ATTITUDE:
Did the individual demonstrate a positive and professional approach to the assignment? Did the individual respond in a positive way to suggestions and guidance? Did the individual seek out additional responsibilities? Did the individual project self-confidence?

	Exceeds Requirements	Meets Requirements	Needs Improvement	Not Applicable
Self-Evaluation:	☐	☐	☐	☐
Evaluator's Rating:	☐	☐	☐	☐

EVALUATOR'S COMMENT:

CLIENT RELATIONS:
Did the individual relate well to this client? Were positive impressions created with this client?

	Exceeds Requirements	Meets Requirements	Needs Improvement	Not Applicable
Self-Evaluation:	☐	☐	☐	☐
Evaluator's Rating:	☐	☐	☐	☐

EVALUATOR'S COMMENT:

DEVELOPMENT OF PERSONNEL:
Did the individual effectively assign available talent to get the work done? Was the individual readily accepted as a leader? Was the individual effective in supervision and in on-the-job training of others?

	Exceeds Requirements	Meets Requirements	Needs Improvement	Not Applicable
Self-Evaluation:	☐	☐	☐	☐
Evaluator's Rating:	☐	☐	☐	☐

EVALUATOR'S COMMENT:

SUPERVISION AND ON-THE-JOB TRAINING RECEIVED BY EVALUATEE:
Describe supervision and O.-J.-T. you received on this engagement.

EVALUATEE'S COMMENT:

EVALUATOR'S COMMENT:

PRACTICE DEVELOPMENT:
Has initiative been shown in developing further MAS, Tax, or Audit engagements? Has individual capitalized upon referral sources resulting from clients (e.g., bankers, attorneys)?

	Exceeds Requirements	Meets Requirements	Needs Improvement	Not Applicable
Self-Evaluation:	☐	☐	☐	☐
Evaluator's Rating:	☐	☐	☐	☐

EVALUATOR'S COMMENT:

MAJOR STRENGTHS WHICH WERE EVIDENT: _____

SUGGESTED GOALS FOR IMPROVEMENT: _____

THIS INDIVIDUAL IS_____ IS NOT_____ READY FOR INCREASED RESPONSIBILITY: EXPLAIN _____

GENERAL COMMENTS OF EVALUATEE: _____

SIGNATURES:
EVALUATEE_____ DATE_____
EVALUATOR_____ TITLE_____ DATE DISCUSSED_____
PARTNER/MANAGER_____ DATE_____

Reprinted with permission of Laventhol & Horwath (Back)

Seidman & Seidman

STAFF EVALUATION REPORT

Return By_____

(OFFICE)

YRS. WITH
S & S_____

NAME _____

NAME OF CLIENT_____

OTHER ACCTG./PUBLIC_____
EXPERIENCE /PRIVATE

NATURE OF ENGAGEMENT _____

DESCRIBE ASSIGNMENT-_____

LENGTH OF ASSIGNMENT (HOURS) _____NUMBER OF STAFF SUPERVISED_____

BEFORE RATING READ INSTRUCTIONS ON REVERSE SIDE	OUTSTANDING	ABOVE AVERAGE	AVERAGE	NEEDS IMPROVEMENT	UN-SATISFACTORY	NO BASIS FOR EVALUATION
A. PERFORMANCE QUALIFICATIONS:						
1. Administration of assignment						
a. Proper planning & organization						
b. Resourcefulness in the development of audit program						
c. Relating scope of work to internal control						
d. Utilization of client personnel						
e. Efficient use of staff						
f. Effective on-the-job training of assistants						
g. Gaining respect of associates						
h. Ability to analyze, evaluate & solve problems						
i. Detection of the need of additional services for practice development						
j. Effective completion of assignment within budgeted time						
2. Working papers & tax returns						
a. Documentation of work performed, including adequate cross referencing						
b. Conformity to S & S manuals & guides						
c. Sound conclusions and explanations						
d. Completeness						
e. Neatness						
f. Legible handwriting						
g. Accuracy						
3. Technical ability						
a. Adherence to generally accepted accounting principles						
b. Auditing / tax sense						
c. Understanding firm accounting & tax releases						
d. Tax preparation / review						
e. Effectiveness with revenue agent						
f. Report preparation						
B. PROFESSIONAL QUALIFICATIONS:						
1. Inquisitiveness						
2. Creativeness						
3. Relations with staff						
4. Maintaining client relationships						
5. Comprehension and interest in business of client						
6. Interest in professional advancement						
7. Advising superiors promptly of problems						
8. Willingness & ability to accept responsibility						
9. Ability to grasp things easily & retain information						
10. Ability to follow instructions						
11. Effectiveness of expression-						
a. English - Oral						
Written						
b. Languages other than English- (SPECIFY)						
Oral						
Written						
12. Work habits						

Adm. 9/1/79

1717-7   (OVER)

Reprinted with permission of Seidman & Seidman (Front)

C. PERSONAL QUALIFICATIONS	CHECK APPLICABLE COLUMN			
	ABOVE AVERAGE	SATIS-FACTORY	REQUIRES IMPROVEMENT	NO BASIS FOR EVALUATION
1. Appearance				
2. Poise				
3. Tact				
4. Personality				
5. Conduct				
6. Cooperation-Appreciation of mutuality of interests- personal and Firm				
7. Attendance & Punctuality				
8. Stability				
9. Initiative				
10. Decisiveness				
11. Judgment				
12. Maturity (In Relation to Age)				
13. Leadership				
14. Integrity				
15. Attitude				
16. Desirable self-confidence				

INSTRUCTIONS

The purpose of this report is to serve as a summary of information relating to the progress of staff. Essentially the objective is to assist you and others in effectively counseling and developing each member of our staff. This permanent record will aid in selecting qualified persons for promotion and in administering a sound evaluation policy. Be mindful of the fact that careful preparation of this report will lead to an honest and impartial appraisal. Staff are to be rated according to job performance during the period specified.

Clarifying comments and recommendations *must* be inserted below for qualifications requiring improvement. Your suggestions for future development will be most helpful. Your opinions with respect to any outstanding performances or attributes will also be beneficial. *This appraisal should be discussed with the staff person.* Compliment on work well done and be constructive in your suggestions in areas where improvement is required.

REMARKS: _____
_____
_____
_____
_____
_____
_____
_____
_____
_____
_____
_____
_____
_____

Overall reaction ☐ Excellent ☐ Satisfactory ☐ Fair ☐ Unsatisfactory

Is this individual now qualified for heavier responsibilities? ☐ Yes ☐ No

(This question does not necessarily relate to promotion)

Can this individual take over this engagement? ☐ Yes ☐ No ☐ Not Sure

Staff person Reaction to Discussion
☐ Receptive
☐ Indifferent
☐ Antagonistic

Date discussed with staff person_____

I would (ask for / accept / prefer not to have) this individual on my engagements hereafter.

In relation to experience the work assigned was
☐ Complex
☐ Moderately difficult
☐ Relatively easy

If worked for you before has individual ☐ Improved ☐ Stood Still ☐ Retrogressed?

Prepared By_____ Approved By_____

(PARTNER, MANAGER OR SUPERVISOR)

Date _____ Date _____

Adm. 9/1/79

1717 8

Reprinted with permission of Seidman & Seidman (Back)

CPA EXAM

The CPA exam ranks among the most difficult of examinations given by any profession in the United States. Only about 20 percent of those who annually sit for the examination pass. Once you do pass and fulfill the other legal requirements of your state, you become a CPA.

Although some people pass all parts of the exam on the first sitting, most do not. If you don't already know, it is an exam for which you must prepare; you cannot just wing it. Many believe that at least 100 hours must be put into preparation.

If you feel confident with your formal education, perhaps a self-study review of the material is all that is necessary. On the other hand, if you missed some portions of instruction (i.e., fund accounting, tax, etc.) because your courses were weak or nonexistent, perhaps you should strongly consider a review course that will teach rather than just review. Many such courses are offered commercially or through your college.

You should attempt to pass the CPA exam as early in your career as possible. Many firms require that you pass in a certain length of time. As time passes, you will assume more responsibility. Social obligations and family and firm responsibilities will make demands on your time. All reduce your available time as well as your desire to study for the exam.

10 POTPOURRI

TURNOVER

Students will frequently ask about the turnover (attrition rate) of a particular firm or office. To be sure, there is and must be turnover in any firm. Not everyone will ascend the promotional ladder to the top. Many not reaching partnership status are eminently qualified but choose alternative careers.

Staff leave public accounting for many reasons including but not limited to (in no particular order):

- Overtime (too much, too little)
- Travel (too much, too little)
- Advancement (too fast, too slow)
- Location (undesirable, desire another)
- Responsibility (too much, not enough)
- Nature of Work (don't like auditing)
- Personality or Management Style Conflicts
    (professional and/or personal disagreements)

- Time/Budgetary Pressures
  (don't like constantly working against the clock)
- Spouse Pressures (service nature of business '
  may cause stress in your family)
- Salary (not high enough in early years
  when compared to industrial counterparts)
- Incompetence (you realize that you are having
  difficulties when dealing with complex
  technical issues)
- Inability to Manage Others (unable or unwilling
  to develop a successful style/manner of
  managing staff)
- Level of Technical Challenges Offered
  (first few years may not stimulate creativity)
- Fabulous Offer from Client
  (may be difficult to turn down the
  short-range gain)
- Decision to Change Careers, etc.
  (grass may appear greener on other side
  of the fence)

To be sure, these and other situations contribute to turnover. Most students view turnover as a negative factor when evaluating a firm. But from the firm's vantage point, losing staff (especially good staff) has both negative and positive characteristics. Loss of good staff is negative because:

- work may be done a little less efficiently
- reassignments of client engagements may place a temporary burden on remaining staff, or
- younger staff may lose a mentor.

On the other hand, the firm may solidify a client relationship or gain the potential of a new engagement if the staff member accepts new employment with a nonclient.

Turnover will average about 20 percent a year which compares very favorably with other professions and industries. Twenty percent is not excessive! Remember that turnover, when managed effectively creates opportunity (client assignments, stepping into a superior's shoes in an "acting" capacity, etc.). In an interview or while visiting an office, you should not ask if there is turnover. There is! You should diplomatically inquire about reasons for turnover. While most turnover is voluntary (staff person decides to leave and accepts an offer with another employer), some turnover is "forced" by the firm. The term "Easter Parade" was coined to describe the practice of building staff levels for the busy season then calling in a number of staff (usually in April) to inform them their services were no longer required. While the unexpected loss of a major client can result in the need to reduce staff, how the firm manages the process can greatly differ. Some areas to consider include whether an outplacement service is offered (someone to assist with resume preparation, job leads, etc.), and whether staff receive adequate warning ("your performance trend must improve over the next few months or perhaps a career change is in order"). No one ever expects to be fired, but it does occur. Knowing the track record of firms regarding the way they manage their practice (anticipating client gains/losses and the impact on manpower planning) and their attitude toward staff outplacement is an important element of the research process.

SPECIALIZATION

Another frequently asked question in an interview is "Can I specialize?" The answer, again, is what you probably want to hear. "Yes!"

If you want to specialize in the fields of tax or consulting, reread Chapter 6. However, if you are asking about industry specialization, follow these suggestions:

- Very few college seniors know they want to spend their career auditing a specific industry. Interviewers who are aware of this usually suggest that you spend some time (usually two years) on the general audit staff before specializing. This is good advice for, if nothing else, it gives you an opportunity to learn (and make your mistakes) before totally entering the area where you want to "make your mark in life."

- If you are truly desirous of specialization, investigate firms and offices prior to your interviews so as not to waste an interviewer's time (i.e., a New York office is not likely to have a large practice in agribusiness nor will a Phoenix office have a large brokerage or manufacturing practice).
- A proper approach to specialization in an interview could be along these lines: "I have a minor in finance and an interest in banking. Someday I think I would like to become an expert in bank auditing." Assuming you know through investigation prior to your interview that the office you are interviewing has a banking practice, you have scored well. On the other hand, if that office does not have a solid banking practice, you may have hurt your chances by your statement. Prior investigation is important!

PROMOTION

It is widely accepted that promotions (and salary increases) in public accounting are based on merit. Each large firm and most smaller firms have an effective performance evaluation system to determine your promotability. Although firms use a variety of staff titles or levels and the term "merit" is somewhat subjective, the following promotion timetable will give you some idea of what to expect as your career develops.

Years of Experience with Firm	Title (Level)	
0	Hire	
1	Staff Accountant	
2	Semi-Senior	
3	Senior	)Combined as)Senior in
4-5	Supervisor	)some firms
5-8	Manager	
8-12	Partner/Principal	

Some firms have policies restricting promotions before a certain time (i.e., three years before becoming a Senior, or Supervisor, etc.).

MBA—YES OR NO

During an interview some students make the mistake of stating, "I'm thinking seriously of continuing my education toward an MBA (or Law degree)." This statement usually leaves an interviewer cold. What does the student mean? Is the student going to attend school full-time in the fall, go part-time, refuse assignments because of overtime or travel conflicts; or is the student merely trying to impress the interviewer with a desire for and willingness to continue learning? Whatever a student's motives, they will come across wrong if approached in this manner.

It would be much better for a student to ask, "What are your thoughts on obtaining an MBA?" Let the interviewer answer. (You then know how to develop your comments.)

Is a Master's degree in Business Administration necessary for success in public accounting? No, it is not! Is it desirable? Yes and no. Leaving the conclusion and decision to you, let's examine a few of the pros and cons of an MBA:

- An MBA will give you more knowledge which can be applied to solving business problems. However, you will probably not be able to use your "extra" knowledge for several years. For the first two years you will be learning and performing the same functions and tasks as a person with a bachelor's degree. But an MBA will definitely assist you in the long run because you will have knowledge that a BA degree-holder does not. An MBA should be able to identify and solve problems on a more sophisticated level.
- An MBA is more mature—usually two years older.
- An MBA will receive higher offers, usually between $3,000 and $10,000 more than a BA degree-holder and will continue to earn more for at least five years. The firm usually expects the MBA to advance faster than the BA who starts at the same time (the starting

salary differential is thereby justified). An MBA is expected to become a manager in 4-5 years; a BA degree holder can become a manager in 5 years, but it is not expected. However, an MBA loses in excess of $60,000 salary while obtaining the advanced degree and could spend more than $20,000 to obtain it depending on the university and housing costs.

• The overwhelming majority of partners and staff currently in public accounting hold BA degrees, not MBAs.

Should you get an MBA? It's up to you. Basically, if you can afford it in terms of time, expense and investment in your future, then obtain an MBA.

Should you decide you want an MBA, try very hard to attend a program with national recognition rather than one offered by the so-called "second-tier" schools. The degree is the same (MBA), but the education is not and interviewers know it. Interviewers also pay less for MBAs from second-tier schools—your premium may be $2,000 to $3,000 in starting salary—if you are even extended an offer. Remember, firms want a return on their larger investment and feel they get a greater return from nationally recognized schools.

The continued existence of second-tier schools may be in jeopardy due to the government funding agencies' continued scrutiny of these institutions in relation to the soaring costs of higher education.

Should you consider first beginning your career right after graduation and then obtaining an MBA at night? It can and is being done, but it is very difficult because of family pressures, social life and travel and overtime conflicts. It is difficult especially when you consider that the business of public accounting (client service) usually takes precedence over class schedules and studies.

WHAT COURSES SHOULD I TAKE?

Frequently a student will wonder what courses to take as electives during senior year. If you truly want to improve yourself in an area in which most accountants are weak, take English composition or other writing courses. It will not look spectacular on your resume, but will help you become a better employee in an area where many are weak. Learn to communicate well both orally and in writing.

You should also consider taking computer courses. Then take finance, economics and last take accounting—assuming that your required courses were complete. In other words, once you are grounded in accounting, broaden yourself.

COMPUTERS

Accounting and computer science have been "married" and the honeymoon continues. The explosive growth of computers in accounting applications that took place over the last 20 years in large corporations is now being repeated in small companies with microcomputers. It will be difficult, if not impossible, for tomorrow's accountants to avoid the use of computers in their daily work.

SMALL SCHOOL— NO INTERVIEWS ON CAMPUS

Not all firms recruit on all campuses. The reasons are numerous but generally revolve around the cost-benefit relationship. If you are in this situation, here are several suggestions:

- Prepare your resume. Call firms and state that you would like an interview at their office because they do not recruit on campus. You will be asked to send a resume. Send it immediately with a cover letter in which you, among other things, state that you will call again on a certain date—usually within five days of receipt of resume. Call and hope for the best. Good Luck!
- Take your campus interview to the firms. Ask your Placement Director or Accounting Department Chairman to arrange a specific date with several firms on which you and other accounting majors in-

terested in public accounting can all go to the firm's office to conduct half-hour interviews. This eliminates expense as a reason for not interviewing and obtains a "campus interview" for you in the firm's office.

There are many other ways you can identify job possibilities:

- In addition to the classified ads, watch for newspaper and professional/trade journal articles on record growth results, mergers, acquisitions, large government contracts and similar stories which may reflect hiring needs.
- Employment agencies are another source. Generally, private search firms do not represent individuals with little or no experience, but they do know which firms are in a hiring mode and may steer you in the proper direction.
- Many professional associations and state CPA societies have active professional education offerings for members and non-members. Consider attending one of these seminars or conferences for the sole purpose of meeting people and developing job leads. This creative approach to "networking" should be well received by potential employers.
- Past employers can provide helpful introductions to prospective employers for you, even if your former part-time job was in no way related to accounting. Remember, *someone* had to review the books or help with the tax returns at "Joe's Bar & Grill" or "Green Thumb Landscaping."
- Finally, let all of your friends and family know of your availability for employment and seek their help in making contacts with employers.

FIVE-YEAR ACCOUNTING PROGRAMS

There is currently a strong movement in academic circles toward a five-year accounting program and even some movement toward separate schools of accounting. There are several factors which contribute to the growth of these movements:

THE PROFESSION

- Increased education is required to make public accounting a "real" profession similar to law and medicine.
- The "accounting body of knowledge" is growing at an explosive rate making it nearly impossible to teach/learn everything during a four-year program.
- The cost of Continuing Professional Education conducted by the firms is exploding rapidly. Firms would like more to be taught by universities.

UNIVERSITIES

- Business schools in many cases are supporting their entire university. While general college enrollments are down, enrollment in business schools is growing—with accounting majors making up a substantial percentage of the total. Faculty is not available in sufficient quantity to handle the influx of students and still maintain the quality of programs. It is therefore becoming necessary to curtail future enrollment by installing entrance criteria for five-year programs which usually are not found in four-year programs or by restricting the number of students eligible for admission to a separate school of accounting.

Taking the above facts into consideration, along with the drastic changes contemplated for higher education in future years and the expected continued demand for accounting majors, a natural consequence will be to increase the number of accounting programs nation-wide. Most increases will take the form of five-year programs because they are necessary and because they are in vogue. However, there is a problem. Many interviewers—even those hiring an abundance of MBAs, strongly believe that graduates will enter the business world technically or emotionally unprepared to handle assignments. Therefore, further training and education are required. In public accounting, this is easy to understand. A college course must teach you the theory of accounts. Each firm, however, has a different policy or procedure for auditing a transaction, a different workpaper format or a different symbol, etc. As it is impossible for a professor to teach all the policies or procedures currently in use, course work is confined to theory. An additional year of college in a five-year program will give you more theory, more computers and possibly more English; but you will not really know more about practical auditing in the day-to-day world.

We ought to give full support to increased academic requirements because everyone benefits—university, student and firm. However, as part of a five-year program, let us also consider the necessity for real-world, practical experience.

A SOLUTION

INTERNSHIPS, similar to those required of the legal and medical professions, could become mandatory as part of the five-year program. The only difference between existing internship practice in public accounting and what is being proposed is that in the proposed solution the internships would be mandatory for graduation. Under this plan, each accounting major would spend one term as a full-time intern.

- Firms would guarantee a sufficient number of positions for accounting majors.
- Universities and faculty would be more confident that their graduates would be better prepared for their careers.
- Students would be better prepared to deal with their career, have a salary for several months and gain valuable information to be used both in their permanent employment interviews and in the classroom.

But most importantly, students will have had real-world, practical experience.

Internships would be offered at the end of the fourth or beginning of the fifth year or between the fourth and fifth year.

Incidentally, the five-year program really is a misnomer. The program, as generally perceived, involves 150 semester hours for graduation, or about 30 semester hours beyond the requirement for a normal bachelor's degree.

As these programs come into being on various campuses across the country, some of the legitimate questions now being raised (i.e., when to enter the program, transfer students, certification, and/or accreditation requirements, etc.) will be answered and solutions will be developed.

FUTURE INTERVIEWING TECHNIQUES

Public accounting currently estimates that the actual cost of hiring one student from a college campus exceeds $4,000, with estimates as high as $9,000. Needless to say, hiring is expensive. With inflation and increasing competitive pressures to hire the best people, these costs will continue to rise rapidly.

To help hold costs down, faculty, placement officers and firms will attempt to devise new means of recruiting. Technology in the form of videophones, TVs, computers and cassettes may be employed to a much greater extent. Internships may play a larger role in future hiring practices. Regardless of the outcome, the challenges of the future will be met.

DRESS

Read *Dress for Success* by John T. Molloy and follow it.

If unable to obtain the book, follow these guidelines: wear a conservative blue or gray suit, white shirt, appropriate tie and recently shined business shoes. Be well-groomed with a conservative hair style. With the exception of a tie, all this also applies to women.

Your appearance will give the interviewer a continuous message. What message do you want him to get?

THE BEGINNING

As you come to the conclusion of this book, you should actually be at the beginning of your interview preparation. We sincerely hope that the suggestions offered throughout have been beneficial. You should be aware of the interview sequence, your need to prepare for your interviews and your need to act as a mature businessperson.

Use of this knowledge is an individual matter. This book does not guarantee success, but you have increased both your knowledge and your odds for success. In the final analysis, however, you are master of your own destiny.

Good Luck!

11 SAMPLE LETTERS AND RESUMES

SAMPLE LETTERS

The following samples will give you an idea of the type of letters you should send and may receive. Please do not quote these or you could be sending the same letter as other students. *Be original!*

CAMPUS INTERVIEW—INVITATION (FIRM)

.

September 15, 19XX

Ms. Mary Smith
123 Oak Lane
City, State 00000

Dear Mary:

During a recent visit to your university, I had an opportunity
to review your resume at the placement office. Because of
your interest in public accounting and your fine record, we
would like to discuss career opportunities at ABC with you.

We will be on campus on October XX, 19XX. Please show
this letter to your placement director who will assign a
mutually convenient time for our meeting.

Enclosed is a brochure describing ABC which I hope you
will find informative.

I look forward to meeting you.

Sincerely,

Personnel Manager

UNSOLICITED RESUME (STUDENT)

September 15, 19XX
123 Oak Lane
City, State 00000

Mr. Jim Brown
Personnel Manager
ABC & Company
123 Debit Boulevard
Denver, Colorado

Dear Mr. Brown:

I am interested in becoming a Staff Accountant in the
Denver office of ABC. Attached for your review is a copy of
my resume from the University of XXXXXX which details
my record of accomplishments.

To demonstrate my desire to begin a career with ABC, I
will call you on September XX to arrange a mutually convenient
time for an interview in your office.

Thank you for your time and effort on my behalf.

Sincerely,

Mary Smith

SOLICITED RESUME (STUDENT)

November 11, 19XX
123 Oak Lane
City, State 00000

Mr. Jim Brown
Personnel Manager
ABC & Company
123 Debit Boulevard
Denver, Colorado

Dear Mr. Brown:

During our November 10 phone conversation, you asked me to send you a copy of my resume. The attached resume details my record of accomplishments at the University of XXXXXX.

I have a sincere desire to begin my career with the Denver office of ABC because of your excellent reputation for professional and personal growth. Dr. Jones of our faculty has also made positive statements about ABC during our many conversations.

I look forward to hearing from you.

Sincerely,

Mary Smith

CAMPUS INTERVIEW—THANK YOU (STUDENT)

September 15, 19XX
123 Oak Lane
City, State 00000

Mr. Jim Brown
Personnel Manager
ABC & Company
123 Debit Boulevard
Denver, Colorado

Dear Mr. Brown:

Just a short note to thank you for sharing your time and knowledge with me during our interview yesterday at XXXXXX University.

I am very impressed with and excited about the opportunities offered by ABC as compared to my other interviews. Please consider me as a candidate.

Looking forward to a positive response, I remain,

Sincerely,

Mary Smith

OFFICE—INVITATION (FIRM)

September 15, 19XX

Ms. Mary Smith
123 Oak Lane
City, State 00000

Dear Mary:

    It was a pleasure meeting with you last Wednesday at the University of XXXXXX. I was very impressed with you and would like you to visit our office in the near future. During your visit you will meet some of the Partners and Staff who make up our Firm. We would like to plan your visit sometime in the near future.

    To arrange your visit with us, please call me collect at

    We will reimburse you for any expenses you incur on your visit.

Sincerely,

Personnel Manager

OFFICE VISIT—REJECTION (FIRM)

September 15, 19XX

Ms. Mary Smith
123 Oak Lane
City, State 00000

Dear Mary:

It was a pleasure meeting you during our recruiting visit last week. I regret to inform you, however, that we will be unable to offer you a position on our staff at this time.

Best wishes for success in your future endeavors.

Sincerely,

Personnel Manager

159

OFFICE VISIT—CONFIRMATION (FIRM)

October 15, 19XX

Ms. Mary Smith
123 Oak Lane
City, State 00000

Dear Mary:

This will confirm the arrangements for you to visit our Denver office on Monday, November 17 at 10:00 a.m.

We are located in the Jones Building on Debit Avenue. Please ask for me upon arrival. We look forward to your visit.

Sincerely,

Personnel Manager

OFFICE VISIT—THANK YOU (STUDENT)

February 22, 19XX
123 Oak Lane
City, State 00000

Mr. Jim Brown
Personnel Manager
ABC & Company
123 Debit Boulevard
Denver, Colorado

Dear Mr. Brown:

I want to take this opportunity to let you know how much I enjoyed my visit to your office on February 12, 19XX. It was a pleasure and very informative. The people I met were true professionals and have qualities I admire.

As we discussed, my interviewing process will not be completed until April 21 and I will be making my decision by April 30. ABC is definitely high on my list of choices. I feel I could reach my career objectives at ABC.

Thank you for your interest in my career. I will not hesitate to call you should any questions arise.

Sincerely,

Mary Smith

OFFICE VISIT—THANK YOU (STUDENT)

Mr. Jim Brown   November 15, 19XX
Personnel Manager   123 Oak Lane
ABC & Company   City, State 00000
123 Debit Boulevard
Denver, Colorado

Dear Mr. Brown:

I want to thank you and the firm for the exciting office visit I had on November 10. While having a great time, I developed a greater understanding for ABC and saw that I could definitely fit into the Denver office.

Professionalism is very high at ABC, yet you made me feel comfortable and at home. Your Firm and office are superior.

I will call you by January 1 with my decision.

* * * OR * * *

I want to express my appreciation for a most enjoyable and informative visit to your office.

The professionalism and friendliness of the people I met and talked with were most impressive as were the opportunities available at ABC. I especially appreciate the flexibility shown by providing me an opportunity to talk with members of your personnel staff. This first-hand information together with the information from the audit staff provided me with fresh insights regarding the accounting profession and ABC.

Sincerely,

Mary Smith

OFFER (FIRM)

October 15, 19XX

Ms. Mary Smith
123 Oak Lane
City, State 00000

Dear Mary:

   All of those who have met you feel that you have the
potential for a very successful career in public accounting.
Accordingly, we would be pleased to have you accept a
position on our staff at an annual salary of $XX,XXX, plus
compensation for overtime.

   I hope that your visit proved to be interesting and
informative and that we have been able to demonstrate the
outstanding opportunity available to you. I am confident that
you would find your association with ABC very challenging and
rewarding. We look forward to hearing from you when you
have reached a decision on our offer.

   If you plan to be in the Denver area during the holidays,
I would be very pleased to have you drop in to our office.

Sincerely,

Personnel Manager

REJECT (FIRM)

October 25, 19XX

Ms. Mary Smith
123 Oak Lane
City, State 00000

Dear Mary:

Thank you for your recent visit to our office. After further consideration of our needs in light of your background, I regret to inform you that we are unable to offer you a position at this time.

We appreciate your interest in our Firm and wish you success in the future.

Sincerely,

Personnel Manager

ACCEPTANCE OF OFFER (STUDENT)

March 15, 19XX
123 Oak Lane
City, State 00000

Mr. Jim Brown
Personnel Manager
ABC & Company
123 Debit Boulevard
Denver, Colorado

Dear Mr. Brown:

I am very pleased to accept your offer of employment on the audit staff of your Denver office at an annual salary of $XX,XXX.

As we discussed on the phone, I plan to begin on September 2, 19XX. I will make every attempt possible to justify your confidence in me.

Thank you for all your help. See you on September 2.

Sincerely,

Mary Smith

DECLINING OFFER (STUDENT)

September 15, 19XX
123 Oak Lane
City, State 00000

Mr. Jim Brown
Personnel Manager
ABC & Company
123 Debit Boulevard
Denver, Colorado

Dear Mr. Brown:

Thank you very much for the interest you have shown in my career. I appreciate the opportunity you have given me to visit with the staff in your office. After very careful consideration, I have decided to begin my career with XYZ firm. I wish continued success to you and everyone in the office.

* * * OR * * *

After careful consideration, I regret to inform you that I have decided to begin my career with another public accounting firm.

Thank you for your time, effort and understanding while I deliberated over this very difficult and important decision. You and the other members of ABC whom I met helped to make my job search an enjoyable and rewarding experience.

I look forward to seeing you again in the near future.

Sincerely,

Mary Smith

REGRETS (FIRM)

December 17, 19XX

Ms. Mary Smith
123 Oak Lane
City, State 00000

Dear Mary:

Thank you for informing us of your decision to accept employment with another firm. We were naturally disappointed because we feel you are the caliber of person who can be successful in public accounting.

I wish you much success in your career. If I can ever help you in any way, please call me.

Sincerely,

Personnel Manager

RESUME

Your resume is a word picture of yourself. It is not only required in most employment situations, but will also help you summarize your thoughts on your past accomplishments and future plans. A good resume will never get you a job, but it may open a door or two for you. A bad resume may slam the door of opportunity in your face.

Write your resume to fit you individually and your personality. However, there are a few "rules" to be followed:

- Emphasize your strengths and minimize or eliminate any shortcomings.
- Be clear, concise (one page in most cases), neat and accurate.
- Design and lay-out your resume so that it is pleasant to the eye, clean and uncluttered.
- Slant the information to be appealing to your readers—a potential employer.
- Use action words wherever possible (i.e., responsible for, duties, elected, accomplished, awarded, knowledge of, familiar with, promoted to, experienced in, supervised, active member, committee chairman, managed, etc.).
- Follow a standard layout: objectives, education, work experience, special accomplishments, personal information and other data. This is the most widely used and accepted layout for a college student's resume. Resumes or experienced job seekers will usually follow the same format, but will place experience before education. Functional format resumes look like you're trying to hide something.
- Photographs don't belong with resumes. It is also unnecessary to list personal information (sex, age, marital status, etc.).
- Your resume need not be typeset (although $40-50 for professional printing seems small after spending $40,000 to $50,000 on your education), but use a good typewriter or letter quality printer (not a dot-matrix printer). Standard 8½" x 11" white, pale

ivory or light gray stock is preferred. Odd sized paper cannot be filed easily and is awkward to handle.
- Proofread carefully for grammar and spelling. Ask 2-3 other people to also proofread.

Following are acceptable examples of resumes. Use them as a guide to develop your own.

JOHN SMITH

CAMPUS ADDRESS
8063 University Drive
Ann Arbor, Michigan 48100
Phone: (555) 555-1234

PERMANENT ADDRESS
352 Sterling Lane
Utica, Michigan 48011
Phone: (555) 555-1111

OBJECTIVE   Summer internship with a CPA firm.

EDUCATION
19XX - 19XX   SCHOOL OF BUSINESS ADMINISTRATION
               UNIVERSITY OF MICHIGAN
               BBA candidate for May 19XX. Expect to complete
               24 hours of Accounting, with additional emphasis
               in Finance. Will sit for CPA exam upon graduation.
               Active member and committee chairman in Beta
               Alpha Psi, Honorary Accounting Fraternity. Tutor,
               intermediate accounting courses. Will participate
               in Accounting Aid Society in winter.
               Present grade point average 3.4 (A = 4.0).

19XX - 19XX   COLLEGE OF LITERATURE, SCIENCE & THE
               ARTS—UNIVERSITY OF MICHIGAN
               Liberal Arts curriculum emphasizing pre-business.
               Active involvement in school newspaper as
               reporter and sports editor. Elected as dormitory
               representative to student council. Participated in
               intramural sports. Grade point average 3.2 (A=4.0).

EMPLOYMENT
SUMMERS
19XX - 19XX   COX CONSTRUCTION CO.   Dearborn, Michigan
               Crew Chief for civil engineering firm. Supervised
               crew of three-man surveying crew. Responsible
               for timely and efficient completion of   assigned
               surveys.

19XX - 19XX   J. L. SMITH STORES   Detroit, Michigan
               Retail shoe sales for two summers. Sold on
               commission.

PERSONAL
BACKGROUND Born in Detroit, Michigan, November 18, 19XX.
               Graduated with honors from Central High School.
               Member of National Honor Society. President of
               church youth group. Interests include: baseball,
               reading and chess. Available for employment May
               15 to August 29, 19XX.

JOHN TEAL

81623 Jacobs Ave.
Rochester, New York 37652
Phone: (555) 555-6320

OBJECTIVE
Challenging career with a CPA firm's audit staff.

EDUCATION
GRADUATE SCHOOL OF BUSINESS
ADMINISTRATION
THE UNIVERSITY OF TEXAS
MBA candidate for May 19XX. Will sit for CPA
exam in May 19XX. Expect to complete 24 hours
of accounting with additional courses in finance
and business law. Member of the Accounting Club.

THE UNIVERSITY OF FLORIDA
BA with distinction in finance, August 19XX.
Honors Convocation, April 19XX. Active in
University of Florida's intramural tennis and
soccer. Dean's List Junior Year.

BUSINESS
EXPERIENCE
19XX - 19XX
LOMBARD COMPANY, Buffalo, New York
Served as accountant for family-owned manufacturing company. Worked with public accountants in
establishing new accounting system adaptable to
computer use. Responsible for all accounts and
acted as intermediary with financial institutions in
dealing with customers. Also worked in plant as
superintendent. Responsible for materials
ordering. Company volume was approximately
$6 million annually.

PERSONAL
BACKGROUND
Born in Rochester, New York. Graduated with
honors from Dover High School. French Academic
Award senior year. Have travelled extensively
throughout Europe and West Africa. Speak
fluent French. Read extensively, especially business
publications.

AVAILABLE:
May 19XX.

171

JOAN GERBER

Campus Address
4320 8th Street
Los Angeles, California 10620
Phone: (555) 555-6801

Permanent Address
12345 Flanders
Newark, New Jersey 36230
Phone: (421) 555-1240

Objective	Public Accounting. Plan to obtain CPA certificate. Eventually interested in tax accounting.
Education 19XX - 19XX	*University of California—Los Angeles* BBA candidate for May 19XX. Expected completion of 24 credit hours in accounting courses. Course work also includes business law, finance, information systems and data processing, marketing, statistics and policy formation and implementation.
Employment Summer 19XX	*Arthur Andersen & Co.* *Los Angeles, California* Interned in tax department. Tax return preparation. Worked on special project evaluating and recommending a more efficient budget allocation method for a network of sports centers. Excellent exposure to research techniques. Very highly evaluated by co-workers.
Winter 19XX	*Accounting Aid Society* *Denver, Colorado* Helped low-income families, elderly people and students file tax returns. Acquired skills in tax procedures and public relations.
Summer 19XX	*Mr. R's* *Denver, Colorado* Dishwasher and potscrubber.
Summer 19XX	*The Malt Shop* *Atlantic City, New Jersey* Salesperson. Promoted to manager. Responsibilities included inventory control, new merchandise ordering, promotion and pricing. Average work week—60 hours.
Personal Background	Born and raised in Newark, New Jersey. Graduated from Canton High School, 17th out of 184. National Honor Society. Member tennis and swim teams. Homeroom treasurer. President Human Relations Club. First female member in school's Kiwanis Club. Enjoy travel and reading.
References	Will be supplied on request.
Available	September 19XX

MARY DAY

Campus Address	*Permanent Address*
842 Dolan Hall	27 Richard Court
Madison, Wisconsin 86212	Chicago, Illinois 73458
Phone: (555) 555-6210	Phone: (555) 555-2680

OBJECTIVE   Career with a Big-8 CPA firm.

EDUCATION
  19XX -XX   *School of·Business*   *The University of Wisconsin*

B.A. Candidate for May 19XX. Broad curriculum in business with emphasis in Accounting while working towards CPA Certificate. Additional studies include Business Data Processing and Cobol Programming and courses in Marketing. Member Beta Alpha Psi, National Honorary Accounting Fraternity. Campus Coordinator of IRS Volunteer Income Tax Assistance Program in 19XX. Intramural football in 19XX. Member of Dean's List in 19XX and 19XX. Received Scholarship in 19XX. A-grade average.

EMPLOYMENT
  Summer 19XX *Danialson, Incorporated*   *Chicago, Illinois*

Purchase & Sales (Internal audit) department of operations. Corrected errors found in this brokerage firm's database. Duties required understanding of trades of stocks, bonds, and options. Constant contact with branch offices and other internal departments was necessary.

  Summer 19XX *A & Q Industries, Inc.*   *Chicago, Illinois*

Computed and compiled information concerning items of inventory to be entered into the computer system. Also helped in the actual loading of the data.

PERSONAL   Single—age 20. Born and raised in the Chicago area. Graduated high school in top 6% of class. Member National Honor Society. Traveled extensively throughout the United States. Snow and water ski.

REFERENCES Available on request.

JOHN RAZIL

2973 State Street
Walton, Michigan 56320
(555) 555-2356

Objective:	Career in Public Accounting.
Education	**GRADUATE SCHOOL OF BUSINESS MICHIGAN STATE UNIVERSITY**
19XX to Present	*Candidate for degree of Master of Business Administration* in June 19XX. Concentration in Accounting. Strong emphasis in Tax Accounting and Finance. Secretary of MBA Association. Member of Beta Alpha Psi. GPA—3.5 (A=4.0).
19XX to 19XX	UNIVERSITY OF MIAMI MIAMI, FLORIDA
	BA degree, March 19XX. Majored in Marketing with additional course work in accounting and personnel. Achieved Dean's List each term. Coordinated major marketing study for local supermarkets for Chairman. Tutor for basic courses. Lettered in baseball four years.
	40% of college expenses earned through summer employment; 60% baseball scholarship.
Experience Summers 19XX to 19XX	SIX FLAGS OVER GEORGIA ATLANTA, GEORGIA
	Host for Gourmet Room Restaurant. Duties included coordination of food orders with the Dining Room Captain, wine service and providing a gracious dining experience for guests. Trained new employees.
Personal Background	Born and raised in New York City. Enjoy traveling, tennis, waterskiing and most participative sports. For personal reasons, must be located in Miami for at least two years.
References	Furnished upon request.

JOHN T. HAMILTON

1243 State Rd.
Phoenix, Arizona 78453
(555) 555-5214

Objective	A position on the audit staff of an accounting firm.
Education	*University of Arizona Graduate School of Business Administration.*

M.B.A. candidate for May, 19XX. Concentration in Finance and Quantitative Methods. Top 10% of class. Awarded full tuition scholarship both years. Beta Alpha Psi president, winter semester, 19XX. Grader for graduate accounting theory courses. GPA 7.5 (A=8.0).

Arizona State University

Bachelor of Science in Business Administration, June, 19XX. Majored in Accounting. Top 1% of class. Selected outstanding male in June graduating class. Inducted into Alumni Honor Society. Appointed to Board of Governors Budget and Finance Committee. Helped organize Business School student government, and served as president junior and senior years. As treasurer of university student government, was responsible for administration of $180,000 student activities budget. Helped organize Beta Alpha Psi chapter. GPA 3.7 (A=4.0).

CPA exam	*Passed May, 19XX, CPA examination*
Employment	*Coopers & Lybrand*　　　　　*Phoenix, Arizona*
Summer 19XX	Interned on the audit staff, examined payments cycle of various clients during preliminary field work. Examined working capital components during year-end field work. Attended staff accountant course.
Hobbies	University of Arizona Numismatic Society. Men's Open Softball League, summers.

HIEBERT LIBRARY

3 6877 00122 4186

───── ORDER FORM ─────

_____ *Interviewing for a Career in Public Accounting* $10.95

_____ *Interviewing for a Career in Health Care* $7.95

Hampton Press
P.O. Box 805
Rochester, Michigan 48063

(313) 852-0980

Please send me _____ copies of the book marked above. I am enclosing $_____ (add $1.50 per copy for postage and handling). Send check or money order in U.S. funds—no cash or C.O.D.s please. Allow 4-6 weeks for delivery.

Name _____

Address _____

City _____ State _____ Zip _____